Web At Speed Fiber Wonders

Web At Speed Fiber Wonders

Maria .M

Noble Publishing

CONTENTS

INDEX 1

1 Chapter 1   3

2 Chapter 2   24

3 Chapter 3   47

4 Chapter 4   70

5 Chapter 5   95

6 Chapter 6   119

7 Chapter 7   142

INDEX

Chapter 1: Introduction to Fiber Optic Technology
1.1 Overview of traditional internet infrastructure
1.2 Introduction to fiber optics and its significance in high-speed internet
1.3 Historical development of fiber optic technology
1.4 Comparison between traditional cables and fiber optics

Chapter 2: The Science Behind Fiber Optics
2.1 Explanation of how fiber optic cables work
2.2 Core components of fiber optics: glass, cladding, and coating
2.3 Role of light in data transmission
2.4 Advantages of fiber optics over traditional copper cables

Chapter 3: Building the Fiber Backbone
3.1 Deployment of fiber optic infrastructure on a large scale
3.2 Challenges and solutions in laying fiber optic cables
3.3 Importance of a robust backbone for high-speed internet
3.4 Real-world examples of successful fiber optic networks

Chapter 4: Connecting Communities: Fiber to the Home (FTTH)
4.1 The concept of bringing fiber directly to individual homes
4.2 Benefits of FTTH for end-users
4.3 Communities with successful FTTH implementations
4.4 Addressing challenges in implementing FTTH projects

Chapter 5: Gigabit Cities and Beyond
5.1 Exploring the concept of Gigabit cities
5.2 Impact of high-speed internet on urban development
5.3 Technological advancements and innovations enabled by fiber optics
5.4 Global examples of cities leading the way in high-speed connectivity

Chapter 6: Fiber Optics in Emerging Technologies
6.1 Role of fiber optics in supporting emerging technologies (5G, IoT, etc.)
6.2 Future applications and possibilities
6.3 Collaboration between fiber optic technology and other cutting-edge innovations
6.4 Potential challenges and considerations for the future

Chapter 7: The Future of Web at Speed
7.1 Predictions for the future of internet speed and connectivity
7.2 Ongoing research and developments in fiber optic technology
7.3 Policy considerations and implications for widespread adoption
7.4 Closing thoughts on the transformative power of high-speed fiber optic internet

Chapter 1

Introduction to Fiber Optic Technology

Fiber optic innovation addresses a noteworthy development in the field of broadcast communications and information transmission. The utilization of light to convey data over slender strands of glass or plastic filaments has altered the manner in which we impart and get to data. This presentation investigates the basic standards, history, parts, and utilizations of fiber optic innovation, featuring its effect on different enterprises and the more extensive scene of current network.

At its center, fiber optic innovation depends on the standards of light engendering and all out inner reflection to send information over significant distances with insignificant sign misfortune. The idea of directing light through a medium traces all the way back to old times, however the coming of fiber optics as a reasonable method for correspondence arose during the twentieth 100 years. The early improvements made ready for the making of a hearty and proficient correspondence foundation that frames the foundation of the present interconnected world.

The essential structure blocks of fiber optic frameworks comprise of optical strands, light sources, locators, and sign handling gear. Optical strands, regularly made of silica glass or plastic, act as the transmission medium. Light sources, like lasers or light-emanating diodes (LEDs), create the optical signs, while identifiers convert these signs once more into electrical data. Signal handling hardware guarantees the trustworthiness and nature of the sent information. Together, these parts structure a modern organization that empowers high velocity, high-limit information move.

The excursion of fiber optic innovation starts with the comprehension of light and its way of behaving. With regards to fiber optics, light is utilized to help data through the center of the optical fiber. The center, with a higher refractive file than the encompassing cladding, works with complete inner reflection, keeping the light to the fiber. This rule of complete inner reflection permits light motions toward cross the fiber with insignificant constriction, guaranteeing that the sent information arrives at its objective with high loyalty.

The historical backdrop of fiber optic innovation is set apart by critical achievements and forward leaps. The idea of involving light for correspondence was proposed by Alexander Graham Ringer in the late nineteenth 100 years. In any case, reasonable execution anticipated progressions in materials and innovation.

During the 1950s and 1960s, analysts took urgent steps in fostering the primary optical strands. The 1970s saw the commercialization of fiber optic correspondence frameworks, with the main overseas fiber optic link being laid in 1988.

One of the vital benefits of fiber optic innovation is its capacity to communicate information over significant distances with negligible sign corruption. Customary copper-based correspondence frameworks experience the ill effects of sign misfortune overstretched distances, requiring intensification and sign recovery. Fiber optics, then again, can send information more than many kilometers without the requirement for continuous sign supporting. This capacity is especially worthwhile for long stretch correspondence, for example, undersea links interfacing landmasses.

The transmission capacity of fiber optic links far surpasses that of customary copper links. This expanded transmission capacity takes into account the transmission of a lot of information at unbelievably high rates. As the interest for information escalated applications, for example, video web based, distributed computing, and computer generated reality keeps on developing, fiber optic innovation arises as a basic empowering influence of the computerized age. The capacity to help high information rates positions fiber optics as a central innovation for the up and coming age of correspondence organizations.

Fiber optic innovation isn't bound to significant distance correspondence. It has turned into an indispensable piece of neighborhood (LANs), metropolitan region organizations (Monitors), and other brief distance correspondence frameworks. Fiber optic links are utilized to interface structures, server farms, and different offices inside a city, giving high velocity and solid network. The arrangement of fiber optics in these conditions adds to the productive and consistent working of present day metropolitan framework.

The utilization of fiber optics reaches out past correspondence to different modern and logical applications. In medication, fiber optic sensors are utilized for negligibly obtrusive diagnostics and imaging. These sensors can be embedded into the body to catch pictures or screen physiological boundaries, diminishing the requirement for intrusive methodology. Moreover, fiber optic innovation assumes a significant part in detecting and checking applications in ventures like aviation, auto, and ecological observing.

The dependability and security of fiber optic correspondence go with it an alluring decision for basic applications, including military and government organizations. Dissimilar to conventional copper links, fiber optics are insusceptible to electromagnetic obstruction (EMI) and radio-recurrence impedance (RFI). This invulnerability improves the security of information transmission, making it moving for unapproved gatherings to catch or alter the data being communicated. Thus, fiber optic innovation is in many cases the favored decision for networks where information security is of fundamental significance.

The natural effect of fiber optic innovation is another viewpoint that separates it from customary specialized techniques. Fiber optics don't need a similar measure of energy for signal transmission as copper-based frameworks. The energy effectiveness of fiber optics, joined with their long life expectancy and recyclability, lines up with the world-wide push towards manageable advances. As the world looks for eco-accommodating answers for address the difficulties of environmental change, fiber optic innovation arises as a capable decision for building tough and energy-effective correspondence organizations.

The sending of fiber optic innovation has not been without challenges. The underlying expenses related with the establishment of fiber optic framework can be significant. Be that as it may, the drawn out benefits, including decreased support costs and expanded unwavering quality, frequently offset the forthright speculation. Furthermore, headways in fiber optic assembling and establishment strategies have added to cost decreases, making fiber optic innovation more open to a more extensive scope of uses and businesses.

The continuous innovative work in fiber optic innovation keep on pushing the limits of what is conceivable. Advancements in materials, like the improvement of empty central elements and photonic gem strands, plan to additional upgrade the presentation of fiber optic frameworks. These progressions open up additional opportunities for speeding up, broadening reach, and investigating novel applications in fields going from quantum correspondence to elite execution figuring.

The fate of fiber optic innovation holds energizing possibilities. As the interest for fast and solid network develops, fiber optics will assume a focal part in molding the correspondence framework of tomorrow. The continuous endeavors to extend fiber optic organizations to underserved regions and the improvement of new advancements, like 5G organizations and the Web of Things (IoT), highlight the proceeded with pertinence and significance of fiber optic innovation in the developing computerized scene.

All in all, fiber optic innovation remains as a demonstration of human creativity and development in the domain of correspondence. From its initial conceptualization to the current day, fiber optics has changed the manner in which we associate, impart, and share data. Its effect stretches out across different businesses, from media communications and medical care to safeguard and then some. As we explore the intricacies of an undeniably interconnected world, fiber optic innovation stays an essential support point, empowering the consistent progression of information and molding the eventual fate of correspondence.

1.1 Overview of traditional internet infrastructure

The customary web foundation frames the foundation of the computerized world, supporting the huge organization of interconnected gadgets, administrations, and clients that characterize the advanced period. This outline digs into the central components, verifiable advancement, key parts, and the difficulties related with conventional web framework.

Understanding the underpinnings of this foundation is fundamental for getting a handle on the intricacies of the computerized scene and valuing the continuous endeavors to improve its capacities.

The starting points of the conventional web framework can be followed back to the ARPANET, a spearheading network created by the US Branch of Safeguard in the last part of the 1960s. The ARPANET intended to make a strong and decentralized correspondence organization, fit for enduring disturbances, like an atomic assault. The reception of parcel exchanging innovation, where information is separated into bundles for productive transmission, laid the preparation for the improvement of a worldwide correspondence organization.

The progress from the ARPANET to the advanced web occurred during the 1980s with the execution of the Transmission Control Convention (TCP) and the Web Convention (IP). These conventions turned into the foundation of the web's engineering, giving a normalized structure to information transmission and tending to. The development of the Internet in the mid 1990s further powered the development of the web, making it open to a more extensive crowd and introducing the time of computerized data and network.

At its center, customary web framework includes an intricate organization of interconnected physical and coherent parts. The actual foundation envelops the substantial components, for example, server farms, servers, switches, and organization links, while the legitimate framework incorporates the conventions, guidelines, and programming that work with correspondence and information trade. Together, these parts structure the mind boggling snare of innovation that empowers the consistent progression of data across the web.

Server farms act as the operational hubs of the customary web framework. These offices house a huge range of servers and systems administration gear, putting away and handling the tremendous volume of information produced and consumed by clients around the world. The essential position of server farms guarantees productive information conveyance and limits inactivity, adding to a responsive and dependable web insight.

Servers assume an essential part in customary web framework, working as the vaults of sites, applications, and computerized content. At the point when clients access a site or utilize an internet based help, their solicitations are handled by servers, which recover and convey the mentioned data. The disseminated idea of servers across server farms overall improves overt repetitiveness and versatility, guaranteeing constant assistance accessibility even notwithstanding equipment disappointments or organization disturbances.

Switches and switches structure the foundation of web availability, coordinating information bundles between various gadgets and organizations. Switches, specifically, assume a pivotal part in deciding the ideal way for information transmission, guaranteeing productive and opportune conveyance.

The progressive construction of the web, with various layers of interconnected switches, empowers worldwide correspondence by directing information through assorted ways to arrive at its objective.

Network links, including fiber optic and copper links, actually associate the different parts of the web framework. Fiber optic links, specifically, have become necessary to significant distance information transmission because of their high data transfer capacity and low sign weakening. The broad organization of undersea links, earthly links, and interconnected networks shapes the multifaceted web that joins landmasses, nations, and districts, working with worldwide correspondence.

The Space Name Framework (DNS) fills in as the web's location book, deciphering comprehensible area names into IP tends to that PCs use to distinguish each other on the organization. DNS assumes a significant part in working on the client experience, permitting people to get to sites and administrations utilizing recognizable space names as opposed to mathematical IP addresses. The appropriated and progressive nature of the DNS upgrades its flexibility and guarantees productive location goal.

Conventions and principles characterize the guidelines and shows administering correspondence on the web. TCP/IP, as referenced prior, is the principal convention suite that empowers dependable and normalized information transmission. Different conventions, for example, Hypertext Move Convention (HTTP) for web correspondence and Record Move Convention (FTP) for document trade, add to the assorted functionalities of the web. Adherence to these conventions guarantees interoperability and consistent correspondence between various gadgets and frameworks.

The conventional web foundation works on a client-server model, where clients, like individual gadgets or end-clients, demand and get administrations from servers. This model has been instrumental in molding the engineering of the web and is appropriate for content conveyance and intelligent applications. Nonetheless, it likewise acquaints difficulties related with versatility, as a flood in client request can strain server assets and effect execution.

Versatility has been difficult for conventional web foundation, especially as the quantity of web clients and the volume of information keep on developing dramatically. Endeavors to address versatility issues incorporate the organization of Content Conveyance Organizations (CDNs) and the advancement of information transmission conventions. CDNs appropriate substance across different servers decisively situated all over the planet, decreasing idleness and working on the speed of content conveyance.

Security is one more basic part of conventional web foundation. The interconnected idea of the web makes it vulnerable to different security dangers, including digital assaults, information breaks, and noxious exercises.

Encryption conventions, firewalls, interruption identification frameworks, and other safety efforts are executed to defend information and guarantee the respectability and classification of data sent over the web.

The idea of the Web of Things (IoT) presents new difficulties and open doors for customary web foundation. As billions of gadgets become associated with the web, going from shrewd apparatuses and wearable gadgets to modern sensors and independent vehicles, the interest for network assets and information handling capacities increments altogether. Tending to the novel prerequisites of IoT, including low-idleness correspondence and huge gadget network, requires continuous headways in foundation plan.

The customary web foundation faces advancing requests regarding velocity, dependability, and proficiency. The appearance of 5G innovation vows to upset web availability by giving higher information speeds, lower idleness, and expanded network limit. The organization of 5G organizations, combined with progressions in equipment and programming, plans to upgrade the general presentation of the conventional web foundation and backing arising advancements like expanded reality, computer generated reality, and independent frameworks.

While customary web foundation has been instrumental in molding the computerized scene, it isn't without its limits. The incorporated idea of the client-server model can prompt bottlenecks, especially during times of popularity. Moreover, worries about information protection, reconnaissance, and the convergence of force in a couple of significant tech organizations have started conversations about elective models and decentralized structures, like the idea of the decentralized web or Web3.

Endeavors are in progress to investigate and execute elective standards that address the deficiencies of customary web foundation. Decentralized advances, including blockchain and circulated record frameworks, mean to enable clients with more prominent command over their information and decrease dependence on concentrated delegates. These developments try to make a more comprehensive and strong web that focuses on protection, security, and client independence.

Taking everything into account, the customary web framework fills in as the groundwork of the interconnected world we possess today. From its unassuming starting points with the ARPANET to the worldwide organization of today, the development of web foundation has been set apart by innovative headways, normalization endeavors, and continuous difficulties. The mix of actual parts, conventions, and norms makes a mind boggling biological system that empowers the consistent progression of data, supporting a horde of utilizations and administrations.

As we plan ahead, the conventional web framework will keep on going through changes to fulfill the needs of a quickly developing computerized scene. Developments in availability, security, and versatility will shape the up and coming age of web foundation.

Whether through the sending of 5G organizations, the ascent of decentralized innovations, or the investigation of new correspondence standards, the development of web foundation stays a dynamic and indispensable piece of the continuous computerized upset.

1.2 Introduction to fiber optics and its significance in high-speed internet

Fiber optics remains at the cutting edge of present day media communications, addressing a progressive innovation that has changed the scene of information transmission and high velocity web. This presentation gives a top to bottom investigation of fiber optics, its essential standards, verifiable turn of events, and its significant importance in empowering fast web network. As we dig into the complexities of fiber optic innovation, we reveal the key factors that make it a foundation in the mission for quicker, more solid web access.

At its center, fiber optics is an innovation that uses the transmission of light through slender strands of glass or plastic filaments to send data. The major rule that underlies fiber optics is the peculiarity of absolute interior reflection. As light goes through the center of an optical fiber, which has a higher refractive file than the encompassing cladding, it goes through rehashed interior reflections. This cycle actually keeps the light profoundly, permitting it to go over significant distances without critical sign misfortune.

The historical backdrop of fiber optic innovation follows its underlying foundations back to the mid twentieth 100 years, with outstanding improvements during the twentieth century laying the basis for its commonsense execution. The idea of directing light through a mechanism for correspondence objects was proposed by people, for example, Alexander Graham Chime. Nonetheless, it was only after the 1950s and 1960s that scientists gained significant headway in making the principal optical filaments.

The commercialization of fiber optic correspondence frameworks occurred during the 1970s, denoting a critical jump forward in the field. The main down to earth fiber optic links were created and conveyed, preparing for the making of another time in media communications. As innovation kept on propelling, the 1980s saw the laying of the principal transoceanic fiber optic link, interfacing landmasses and exhibiting the worldwide capability of this creative innovation.

The meaning of fiber optics in the domain of high velocity web couldn't possibly be more significant. Conventional techniques for information transmission, for example, copper-based frameworks, experience restrictions regarding data transfer capacity and sign corruption over significant distances. Fiber optics, then again, gives an answer for these difficulties. The capacity of light to convey data over meager strands with insignificant misfortune makes fiber optic innovation the best contender for conveying the high information rates requested by present day web applications.

One of the essential benefits of fiber optics with regards to high velocity web is its unbelievable transfer speed capacities. Dissimilar to copper links, which have a restricted limit with regards to information transmission, fiber optic links can convey an essentially bigger measure of information because of the great recurrence of light waves. This expanded transmission capacity is pivotal for supporting the always developing interest for information escalated applications, for example, streaming, distributed computing, and augmented reality.

The speed at which information goes through fiber optic links is one more key figure their importance for rapid web. Light, as the mode of transmission, goes at a speed near the most extreme feasible in a vacuum. This close light-speed transmission brings about negligible dormancy, giving clients quicker reaction times while getting to online substance or participating continuously applications. The low inertness of fiber optics is particularly basic for applications like internet gaming, video conferencing, and other intuitive encounters.

Fiber optics assumes a vital part in tending to the difficulties presented by the "last mile" issue in web network. The last mile alludes to the last leg of the broadcast communications network that associates the specialist co-op's framework to the end-client's area. In conventional copper-based frameworks, the last mile frequently turns into a bottleneck, prompting decreased paces and unwavering quality. Fiber optics, with its capacity to send a lot of information over significant distances without signal corruption, mitigates the constraints related with the last mile, guaranteeing that clients experience reliable rapid web access.

The arrangement of fiber optics isn't restricted to significant distance correspondence; it reaches out to nearby organizations, metropolitan regions, and even inside structures. Fiber optic links are utilized to make fast, dependable associations in neighborhood (LANs) and metropolitan region organizations (Monitors). The execution of fiber optics in these settings adds to the productive working of present day metropolitan foundation, supporting organizations, instructive establishments, and different associations that depend on consistent availability.

The dependability and power of fiber optic innovation settle on it a favored decision for basic applications past shopper web access. Ventures like medical care, money, and government influence fiber optics for secure and high-data transmission correspondence. In medical services, for instance, fiber optic sensors are utilized for clinical imaging and diagnostics, giving a harmless method for observing patients. The inborn security of fiber optics, which is insusceptible to electromagnetic obstruction, makes it appropriate for applications where information trustworthiness and privacy are central.

The security and flexibility of fiber optic correspondence are especially pertinent in military and government organizations. Conventional copper links are vulnerable to electromagnetic impedance and snoopping, making them less secure for sending delicate data. Fiber optics, by excellence of its invulnerability to such obstruction, improves the security of information transmission, guaranteeing that basic interchanges stay private and positive.

The natural effect of fiber optic innovation is another perspective that lines up with the worldwide push towards manageable arrangements. Fiber optics are more energy-productive contrasted with conventional copper-based frameworks, requiring less power for signal transmission. Also, the life span and recyclability of fiber optic links add to decreasing the ecological impression of correspondence foundation. As the world progressively looks for eco-accommodating other options, fiber optics arise as a mindful decision for building energy-effective and reasonable fast web organizations.

Notwithstanding its various benefits, the broad reception of fiber optics has experienced difficulties. The underlying expenses related with the establishment of fiber optic framework can be critical, representing a boundary to passage for certain districts and networks. Notwithstanding, the drawn out benefits, including lower upkeep costs and higher unwavering quality, frequently offset the forthright venture. Besides, progressions in fiber optic assembling and establishment procedures keep on driving down costs, making fiber optic innovation more available to a more extensive scope of uses.

Continuous innovative work in fiber optic innovation plan to push the limits of what is conceivable. Advancements in fiber optics incorporate the improvement of cutting edge fiber types, like empty central elements and photonic precious stone filaments. These advancements hold the possibility to additional improve the exhibition of fiber optic frameworks, offering sped up, expanded reach, and novel applications in arising fields like quantum correspondence and elite execution processing.

The eventual fate of fiber optic innovation is portrayed by interesting potential outcomes and proceeded with development. As the interest for fast and solid availability develops, fiber optics will stay at the very front of molding the correspondence framework of tomorrow. Drives to grow fiber optic organizations to underserved regions, combined with the arrangement of cutting edge advancements, for example, 5G, feature the continuous significance and significance of fiber optic innovation in the consistently developing computerized scene.

1.3 Historical development of fiber optic technology

The verifiable improvement of fiber optic innovation is an excursion set apart by diligent development, historic disclosures, and mechanical jumps that have reshaped the scene of media communications. This investigation digs into the key achievements, persuasive figures, and groundbreaking minutes that have molded the advancement of fiber optics from its reasonable beginnings to the broad reception and incorporation into present day correspondence organizations.

The underpinnings of fiber optic innovation can be followed back to the late nineteenth hundred years, where the idea of involving light for correspondence was first proposed. Alexander Graham Ringer, known for his creation of the phone, imagined the chance of sending sound utilizing light waves.

Despite the fact that Ringer's photophone explore in 1880 exhibited the transmission of sound on a light emission, reasonable execution anticipated the mechanical headways of the twentieth hundred years.

The genuine birth of fiber optic innovation happened during the 1950s and 1960s with the improvement of the principal useful optical filaments. Early trials included directing light through straightforward materials, yet it was only after 1954 that physicist Harold Hopkins and Narinder Singh Kapany, an Indian-conceived American physicist, begat the expression "fiber optics" in a logical paper. Their work established the groundwork for the ensuing progressions in fiber optic correspondence.

In 1960, physicist Elias Snitzer made a basic forward leap by showing the main optical fiber with low sign misfortune. Snitzer's work at American Optical Organization prompted the formation of a glass fiber fit for communicating light signals over significant distances with negligible lessening. This obvious a vital second in the possibility of commonsense fiber optic correspondence frameworks.

The year 1966 saw another huge improvement when Charles K. Kao, a physicist and electrical designer, distributed a notable paper that would procure him the Nobel Prize in Material science in 2009. Kao's paper centered around the capability of involving glass filaments for optical correspondence and recognized the vital test of lessening signal misfortune. His visionary work laid the foundation for the reasonable acknowledgment of significant distance fiber optic correspondence.

The leap forwards of the 1960s made ready for the principal functional fiber optic framework. In 1970, specialists Donald Keck, Peter Schultz, and Robert Maurer at Corning Glass Works fostered the main low-misfortune optical fiber. This development, known as "Corning 1," had a deficiency of 17 decibels for every kilometer, a critical improvement over prior filaments. The production of Corning 1 denoted a pivotal achievement in making fiber optic correspondence economically practical.

Following the advancement of low-misfortune optical filaments, the 1970s saw the primary functional executions of fiber optic correspondence frameworks. In 1977, the primary live phone traffic was sent through a fiber optic framework in Lengthy Ocean side, California. This memorable second shown this present reality capability of fiber optics for broadcast communications and set up for its fast extension in the next many years.

The 1980s denoted a time of broad reception and commercialization of fiber optic innovation. The primary transoceanic fiber optic link, TAT-8, was laid in 1988, associating the US and Europe. This link, traversing north of 3,000 miles, showed the possibility of involving fiber optics for long stretch correspondence across landmasses. The progress of TAT-8 made ready for a worldwide organization of undersea fiber optic links.

All the while, fiber optic innovation started to supplant conventional copper-based correspondence frameworks in different applications. The benefits of fiber optics, for example, higher data transmission and lower signal misfortune, turned out to be progressively clear. As interest for high velocity and dependable correspondence developed, fiber optics arose as the favored decision for significant distance and high-limit information transmission.

The 1990s saw the fast extension of fiber optic organizations, driven by the hazardous development of the web. The Internet, which had arisen in the mid 1990s, filled an extraordinary interest for information transmission abilities. Fiber optics turned into the foundation of the web framework, empowering the consistent trade of data across the globe. The sending of fiber optic links in metropolitan regions and metropolitan focuses added to the foundation of rapid web network.

Progressions in fiber optic innovation during the late twentieth century zeroed in on expanding information transmission rates and tending to difficulties like scattering and sign recovery. The presentation of frequency division multiplexing (WDM) during the 1990s permitted different signs to be sent all the while over a solitary optical fiber, essentially expanding the general limit of fiber optic correspondence frameworks.

The mid 21st century saw the proceeded with refinement and development of fiber optic innovation. Thick frequency division multiplexing (DWDM) further expanded the limit of optical strands by thickly pressing various frequencies of light. This innovation assumed a vital part in satisfying the raising need for transmission capacity, particularly in long stretch correspondence and high-traffic network courses.

As fiber optic organizations turned out to be more inescapable, research endeavors moved towards investigating new sorts of optical strands with upgraded execution attributes. Empty central elements, for instance, were created to decrease signal contortion brought about by communications with the glass material. Photonic gem filaments, with their interesting design, offered extra command over light spread and scattering, opening up additional opportunities for fitting fiber optic properties to explicit applications.

The mid-2010s saw another period of development with the rise of room division multiplexing (SDM). SDM includes communicating numerous information streams at the same time utilizing different spatial modes inside a solitary optical fiber. This approach vows to additional increment the limit of fiber optic correspondence frameworks, tending to the always developing interest for higher information rates.

The verifiable improvement of fiber optic innovation is portrayed by a ceaseless pattern of development, from the conceptualization of involving light for correspondence to the viable execution of high-limit, rapid fiber optic organizations. The extraordinary effect of fiber optics reaches out past broadcast communications, affecting different ventures and applications.

The meaning of fiber optics in current media communications lies in its capacity to give unrivaled information transmission abilities. Fiber optic links are the foundation of significant distance correspondence, empowering the interconnection of mainlands through undersea links. These links, extending huge number of kilometers across the sea floor, represent the dependability and effectiveness of fiber optic innovation in defeating the constraints of customary correspondence frameworks.

The arrangement of fiber optics in metropolitan and metropolitan regions has changed nearby correspondence organizations. Fiber optic links associate server farms, organizations, instructive establishments, and local locations, framing the foundation that upholds rapid web access. The consistent transmission of information over fiber optics is crucial to the working of current cultures, empowering exercises going from online training and remote work to web based business and diversion.

Fiber optic innovation has likewise tracked down applications past conventional media communications. In medical care, fiber optic sensors are utilized for clinical imaging and diagnostics. These sensors, equipped for sending light through the human body, give a harmless method for observing physiological boundaries and catching pictures for symptomatic purposes.

In modern settings, fiber optics assume a pivotal part in detecting and checking applications. Fiber optic sensors are utilized for estimating boundaries like temperature, tension, and strain in conditions where customary sensors might be illogical or vulnerable to obstruction. This flexibility makes fiber optics important in businesses going from aviation and car to oil and gas.

The security and unwavering quality of fiber optic correspondence settle on it an optimal decision for applications where information honesty is of most extreme significance. Military and government networks influence fiber optics to guarantee secure and strong correspondence. The insusceptibility of fiber optics to electromagnetic impedance and snoopping improves the privacy of communicated data, making it a favored innovation for strategic applications.

The natural effect of fiber optic innovation adds to its importance with regards to reasonable framework. Fiber optics are energy-effective contrasted with customary copper-based frameworks, requiring less power for signal transmission. Furthermore, the life span and recyclability of fiber optic links line up with the worldwide push towards eco-accommodating arrangements, settling on fiber optics a mindful decision for building energy-effective and naturally cognizant correspondence organizations.

Looking forward, the verifiable improvement of fiber optic innovation fills in as a demonstration of human resourcefulness and the persevering quest for development. As we stand at the cliff of the following rush of mechanical progressions, fiber optics keeps on assuming a focal part in molding the fate of correspondence.

Continuous innovative work endeavors center around pushing the limits of fiber optic abilities, investigating new materials, and opening novel applications that will additionally move the advancement of this extraordinary innovation.

1.4 Comparison between traditional cables and fiber optics

The correlation between customary links, frequently founded on copper, and fiber optics is a critical investigation in the domain of broadcast communications and information transmission. This examination dives into the principal distinctions, benefits, and constraints of every innovation, revealing insight into the elements that make fiber optics a groundbreaking power in current correspondence organizations.

Customary links, generally dependent on copper as the transmission medium, have been the foundation of correspondence frameworks for a really long time. Copper links are known for their strength and conductivity, making them appropriate for sending electrical signs. Nonetheless, as innovation progressed and the interest for higher information rates and longer distances expanded, copper links started to uncover specific impediments.

One of the essential differentiations between conventional copper links and fiber optics lies in the transmission medium. Copper links communicate electrical signs utilizing electrical flows, while fiber optics use light signals sent through slender strands of glass or plastic filaments. This central contrast has extensive ramifications for the exhibition, transfer speed, and proficiency of the two advancements.

Transfer speed, frequently portrayed as the information conveying limit of a correspondence station, is a basic boundary in the examination between conventional links and fiber optics. Copper links have restricted data transfer capacity abilities, particularly over significant distances. As signs travel through copper, they experience weakening, prompting signal misfortune and diminished data transmission. Fiber optics, then again, outfit the high recurrence of light waves, empowering them to convey a fundamentally bigger measure of information over more noteworthy distances with negligible sign corruption.

The effectiveness of information transmission is a vital thought in the correlation between copper links and fiber optics. Copper links are powerless to electromagnetic impedance (EMI) and radio-recurrence obstruction (RFI). Outside variables, for example, close by electrical cables, electronic gadgets, and ecological circumstances can present commotion and twist signals in copper links, prompting a lessening in signal quality. Interestingly, fiber optics are safe to EMI and RFI, giving a protected and obstruction free transmission medium.

Distance is a vital figure assessing the presentation of correspondence frameworks, particularly in significant distance correspondence or undersea link establishments. Conventional copper links face restrictions in signal lessening overstretched distances, requiring the utilization of sign repeaters or speakers to keep up with signal honesty.

Fiber optics, with their low sign lessening attributes, can send information over significantly longer distances without the requirement for successive sign recovery. This benefit is especially apparent in undersea links associating mainlands, where fiber optics have turned into the favored decision for high-limit, significant distance correspondence.

One more basic angle in the examination between copper links and fiber optics is signal honesty. As signs travel through copper links, they are helpless to contortion and sign misfortune because of variables, for example, impedance bungle and ecological obstruction. Fiber optics, with their resistance to outside obstruction and low sign misfortune, guarantee reliable sign trustworthiness even in testing conditions. This trademark is fundamental for applications where information exactness and unwavering quality are central.

The weight and size of transmission links assume a huge part in different applications, from aviation to media communications framework. Copper links are for the most part heavier and bulkier contrasted with fiber optic links. The lightweight and minimized nature of fiber optic links add to more straightforward establishment, diminished actual stress on help structures, and expanded adaptability in sending correspondence organizations. This benefit turns out to be especially pertinent in situations where space and weight imperatives are basic contemplations.

Security contemplations additionally recognize fiber optics from conventional copper links. Copper links emanate electromagnetic signs that can be captured, prompting potential security weaknesses. Fiber optics, sending light signals inside a glass or plastic center, are safer as they don't emanate perceptible signs that can be effectively captured. This innate security highlight goes with fiber optics a favored decision for applications where information privacy is vital.

The natural effect of transmission advancements is an undeniably significant figure the present setting of manageability. Copper mining and extraction processes have huge natural ramifications, including living space interruption and water contamination. Fiber optics, made fundamentally from silica glass, add to a more modest natural impression. The life span and recyclability of fiber optic links further line up with worldwide endeavors to embrace eco-accommodating innovations and decrease electronic waste.

Cost contemplations frequently impact innovation decisions in the sending of correspondence organizations. By and large, customary copper links have been leaned toward for their lower beginning establishment costs. In any case, the all out cost of responsibility for life pattern of an organization can uncover an alternate picture. Fiber optic links, notwithstanding higher beginning expenses, offer benefits, for example, lower support costs, diminished energy utilization, and longer life expectancy. As fiber optic innovation keeps on propelling, the expense uniqueness between customary links and fiber optics is slowly decreasing, making fiber optics an undeniably financially savvy arrangement over the long haul.

The adaptability of fiber optic innovation reaches out past conventional information transmission. Fiber optics are appropriate for different applications, including the transmission of voice, video, and information. The utilization of fiber optics in clinical applications, detecting advancements, and modern conditions features the flexibility and multifunctionality of this innovation. Customary copper links, essentially intended for electrical sign transmission, may confront difficulties in gathering the assorted necessities of current correspondence frameworks.

The fast progressions in fiber optic innovation have prompted the advancement of particular fiber types and setups, each customized to explicit applications. Empty main elements, for example, intend to alleviate signal bending brought about by cooperations with the glass material. Photonic precious stone strands offer extra command over light proliferation, opening up additional opportunities for customization. These advancements grandstand the powerful idea of fiber optics, consistently developing to meet the advancing necessities of assorted enterprises and applications.

2

Chapter 2

The Science Behind Fiber Optics

Fiber optics is an entrancing and progressive innovation that has changed the manner in which we impart, communicate information, and interface with the world. At its center, fiber optics depends on the standards of light spread through meager strands of glass or plastic filaments. The science behind fiber optics is a mind boggling and interdisciplinary field that includes physical science, materials science, optics, and media communications. In this investigation, we will dig into the basic standards, parts, and utilizations of fiber optics, revealing insight into the science that supports this wonderful innovation.

At the core of fiber optics is the idea of all out interior reflection, a peculiarity that happens while light going through a thick medium experiences a limit with a less thick medium at a point more prominent than the basic point. With regards to fiber optics, the thick medium is the center of the optical fiber, and the less thick medium is the encompassing cladding. The center and cladding materials are painstakingly decided to guarantee that the basic point is surpassed, permitting light to be bound to the center through numerous reflections.

The center of an optical fiber is normally made of glass or plastic, picked for its straightforwardness and capacity to send light effectively. Glass filaments, specifically, are broadly utilized because of their low sign misfortune and high transmission capacity abilities. The cladding, encompassing the center, has a lower refractive record to work with all out inside reflection. Keeping up with this basic point is significant for forestalling signal misfortune and guaranteeing the effective transmission of information over significant distances.

One of the critical benefits of fiber optics over customary copper-based correspondence frameworks is its capacity to convey information over significant distances with insignificant sign misfortune. Copper links experience the ill effects of sign debasement over distance because of opposition and different variables. Conversely, optical strands experience essentially lower signal weakening, permitting information to be sent north of many kilometers without the requirement for successive sign intensification.

The most common way of directing light through an optical fiber includes a few parts, including light sources, modulators, and locators. Light-transmitting diodes (LEDs) and lasers are normal light sources utilized in fiber optic frameworks. These sources create light signals that are then balanced to encode information. The balance cycle includes differing the force or recurrence of the light sign to address double information. This tweaked light sign is then communicated into the optical fiber for proliferation.

As light goes through the fiber, it goes through scattering, a peculiarity where various frequencies of light travel at various paces. This scattering can prompt sign contortion, restricting the bandwidth of the fiber. To resolve this issue, different scattering the executives strategies are utilized, like utilizing various kinds of strands or acquainting repaying components with check the impacts of scattering.

Fiber optics tracks down far reaching application in media communications, where fast information transmission is essential. The utilization of optical filaments in media transmission networks has upset the web, empowering the quick and solid exchange of huge measures of information. Fiber optic links are likewise widely utilized in digital broadcasting companies, giving top notch video and sound transmission. The high data transmission and low sign misfortune qualities of fiber optics pursue it an optimal decision for these applications.

Notwithstanding broadcast communications, fiber optics assumes an imperative part in clinical imaging and detecting innovations. Endoscopes, for instance, use fiber optic groups to communicate light into the body and catch pictures for demonstrative purposes. The adaptability and little size of optical filaments make them appropriate for applications where conventional imaging strategies might be illogical or obtrusive.

One more charming part of fiber optics is its application in sensors and estimation gadgets. Fiber optic sensors can recognize changes in temperature, tension, and strain by estimating the varieties in light force or stage. These sensors are broadly utilized in ventures like aviation, medical care, and natural observing. The inborn resistance of optical strands to electromagnetic obstruction makes them especially worthwhile in conditions where conventional sensors might be vulnerable to outer impacts.

The organization of fiber optic links has reformed correspondence as well as prepared for cutting edge innovations, for example, fiber optic detecting organizations and circulated acoustic detecting (DAS). DAS uses the capacity of optical strands to identify acoustic signs along their length. By dissecting changes in light examples brought about by acoustic aggravations, DAS frameworks can be utilized for applications, for example, pipeline observing, border security, and seismic discovery.

The advancement of fiber optic innovation has prompted the improvement of different kinds of optical filaments, each custom fitted to explicit applications. Single-mode filaments, with a little center width, are intended for significant distance correspondence and high velocity information transmission. Multimode filaments, then again, have a bigger center measurement and are reasonable for more limited distance correspondence inside structures or grounds.

The assembling system of optical filaments includes exact control of the materials and aspects to accomplish ideal light transmission properties. The preform, a tube shaped glass pole, fills in as the beginning stage for fiber creation.

The preform is warmed and extended to make a slim fiber with the ideal center and cladding aspects. The subsequent fiber is then covered to safeguard its surface and upgrade its mechanical strength.

The mission for higher transfer speed and quicker information transmission has driven the improvement of new advancements inside the field of fiber optics. One such headway is frequency division multiplexing (WDM), a strategy that empowers the synchronous transmission of numerous frequencies (or shades) of light through a solitary optical fiber. Every frequency can convey its own free information stream, really expanding the general information limit of the fiber.

WDM innovation comes in two primary structures: coarse frequency division multiplexing (CWDM) and thick frequency division multiplexing (DWDM). CWDM utilizes a more extensive dividing between frequencies, considering fewer channels. Conversely, DWDM uses firmly stuffed frequencies, empowering a lot bigger number of channels and, subsequently, more noteworthy information limit. WDM plays had a pivotal impact in fulfilling the steadily developing need for higher information rates in current correspondence organizations.

Past WDM, specialists are investigating new boondocks in fiber optic innovation, including the improvement of empty main elements. Dissimilar to customary strong central elements, these strands have a center that is to some degree or completely made of air or another low-file material. Empty main elements offer novel benefits, for example, lower signal scattering and the potential for sending light in a more extensive scope of frequencies.

The study of fiber optics stretches out past the transmission of information; it additionally envelops the field of optical enhancement.

Optical enhancers are gadgets that support the strength of optical signs without switching them over completely to electrical signs. Erbium-doped fiber speakers (EDFAs) are generally utilized in significant distance optical correspondence frameworks. These speakers contain a modest quantity of erbium particles in the fiber center, which can be optically siphoned to enhance signals at explicit frequencies.

The advancement of fiber optic innovation has not been without challenges. One eminent snag is the weakening of sign strength because of different variables, including assimilation, dissipating, and twisting misfortunes. Specialists consistently work to work on the materials and plan of optical strands to limit these misfortunes and improve signal respectability. Furthermore, the expense of assembling and sending fiber optic organizations stays a thought, in spite of the fact that headways underway methods have relieved this worry over the long haul.

As the interest for higher information rates and more dependable correspondence keeps on developing, specialists are investigating imaginative answers for stretch the boundaries of fiber optic innovation.

One such area of investigation is the field of quantum optics, where the standards of quantum mechanics are applied to control and communicate data utilizing individual photons. Quantum correspondence utilizing fiber optics holds the commitment of super secure correspondence channels, as any endeavor to capture the quantum condition of a photon would be discernible.

The study of fiber optics is likewise interwoven with the investigation of nonlinear optics, where the way of behaving of light inside a medium is impacted by its power. Nonlinear impacts can be both a test and an open door in fiber optics. On one hand, nonlinearities can cause signal mutilation and breaking point the transmission distance. Then again, they can be outfit for applications like optical exchanging and recurrence change.

All in all, the science behind fiber optics addresses an enamoring combination of physical science, materials science, and designing. The capacity to send information at the speed of light through slight strands of glass has reformed correspondence, network, and different mechanical applications. From the standards of all out inside reflection to the improvement of cutting edge optical filaments and enhancement strategies, fiber optics keeps on being a main thrust in forming the manner in which we see and cooperate with the world. As scientists push the limits of innovation, the fate of fiber optics holds the commitment of considerably quicker information transmission, expanded transfer speed, and novel applications that will additionally change the scene of correspondence and innovation.

2.1 Explanation of how fiber optic cables work

Fiber optic links are a wonder of current innovation, empowering the rapid transmission of information over significant distances with negligible sign misfortune. At the center of their usefulness lies the material science of light spread and the cunning plan of the optical strands that comprise these links. Understanding how fiber optic links work requires an investigation of the key standards, parts, and cycles associated with their activity.

The crucial rule that oversees the activity of fiber optic links is complete inside reflection. This peculiarity happens while light going through a medium with a higher refractive file experiences a limit with a lower refractive record at a point more noteworthy than the basic point. With regards to fiber optics, the high refractive file medium is the center of the optical fiber, and the low refractive record medium is the encompassing cladding.

The center of an optical fiber is commonly made of glass or plastic, picked for its straightforwardness and capacity to proficiently send light. Glass filaments, specifically, are generally utilized because of their low sign misfortune and high data transmission capacities. The cladding, which encompasses the center, has a lower refractive record, guaranteeing that light inside the center goes through all out inner reflection.

Absolute inward reflection keeps the light to the center of the optical fiber, permitting it to go along the length of the fiber through various reflections. This restriction is essential for forestalling signal misfortune and keeping up with the trustworthiness of the sent information. The whole construction of the optical fiber, including the center and cladding, is intended to guarantee that the basic plot for absolute interior reflection is surpassed.

The most common way of directing light through an optical fiber includes a few key parts. The light source, frequently a laser or light-radiating diode (Drove), creates the underlying light sign. This sign is then balanced to encode information, with varieties in force or recurrence addressing paired data. The regulated light sign is coupled into the optical fiber, where it goes through the course of complete interior reflection and goes along the length of the fiber.

As the light sign engenders through the fiber, it might experience scattering, a peculiarity where various frequencies of light travel at various velocities. Scattering can prompt sign contortion, restricting the bandwidth of the fiber. To relieve this impact, different scattering the executives procedures are utilized, including the utilization of specific strands or the presentation of remunerating components.

The plan of fiber optic links likewise thinks about the issue of sign lessening, where the strength of the light sign decreases as it goes through the fiber. Dissimilar to customary copper-based links, which experience the ill effects of huge sign misfortune over significant distances, optical strands experience a lot of lower constriction. This trademark permits fiber optic links to communicate information north of many kilometers without the requirement for successive sign intensification.

The enhancement of optical signs in fiber optic links is accomplished using optical speakers, with erbium-doped fiber intensifiers (EDFAs) being a typical decision. These speakers contain a limited quantity of erbium particles in the fiber center, which can be optically siphoned to enhance signals at explicit frequencies. Optical enhancers assume a significant part in expanding the range of optical correspondence frameworks and making up for signal misfortunes.

The arrangement of fiber optic links has upset broadcast communications, giving the spine to rapid web, phone organizations, and satellite

TV. The benefits of fiber optics, like high transmission capacity, low sign misfortune, and invulnerability to electromagnetic impedance, settle on them an optimal decision for sending immense measures of information over significant distances.

Notwithstanding broadcast communications, fiber optic links track down applications in different fields, including clinical imaging, detecting advances, and modern applications. Fiber optic sensors, for instance, can recognize changes in temperature, tension, or strain by estimating varieties in light power or stage. The adaptability and little size of optical filaments make them appropriate for applications where customary sensors might be illogical.

The assembling system of optical filaments includes a few moves toward guarantee exact control of materials and aspects. The beginning stage is the preform, a barrel shaped glass bar that fills in as the establishment for the fiber. The preform is warmed and extended to make a slender fiber with the ideal center and cladding aspects. The subsequent fiber is then covered to safeguard its surface and improve its mechanical strength.

The persistent mission for higher information rates and expanded transmission capacity has prompted progressions in fiber optic innovation, including the advancement of frequency division multiplexing (WDM). WDM permits various frequencies, or varieties, of light to be sent at the same time through a solitary optical fiber. This method really expands the general information limit of the fiber, tending to the developing interest for quicker and more effective correspondence organizations.

Two primary types of WDM are generally utilized: coarse frequency division multiplexing (CWDM) and thick frequency division multiplexing (DWDM). CWDM utilizes more extensive dispersing between frequencies, obliging fewer channels. Interestingly, DWDM uses firmly stuffed frequencies, empowering a lot larger number of channels and, therefore, more noteworthy information limit. WDM has turned into a foundation innovation in present day optical correspondence organizations.

The development of fiber optic innovation has likewise seen the rise of empty central elements as a clever plan. Dissimilar to conventional strong central elements, empty main elements have a center that is somewhat or completely made of air or another low-file material. This plan offers extraordinary benefits, including lower signal scattering and the potential for sending light in a more extensive scope of frequencies.

Regardless of the various benefits of fiber optics, the innovation isn't without its difficulties. One huge obstruction is the lessening of sign strength, which can result from different elements, including ingestion, dissipating, and twisting misfortunes. Continuous innovative work endeavors center around working on the materials and plan of optical filaments to limit these misfortunes and upgrade generally speaking sign trustworthiness.

The expense of assembling and sending fiber optic organizations has been a thought, in spite of the fact that headways underway strategies have added to cost relief over the long haul. As fiber optic innovation keeps on propelling, specialists investigate new wildernesses, like the reconciliation of quantum optics standards into fiber optics. Quantum correspondence utilizing fiber optics holds the commitment of super secure correspondence channels, utilizing the standards of quantum mechanics to send data with uncommon security.

The investigation of nonlinear optics is one more area of investigation inside the domain of fiber optics. Nonlinear impacts, where the way of behaving of light is impacted by its force, can be both a test and an open door.

While nonlinearities can cause signal twisting and breaking point transmission distances, they can likewise be outfit for applications like optical exchanging and recurrence transformation.

2.2 Core components of fiber optics: glass, cladding, and coating

Fiber optics, a progressive innovation that supports current correspondence frameworks, depends on the mind boggling interchange of center parts inside its design. At the core of this innovation are three fundamental components: the glass center, cladding, and covering. Understanding the properties and jobs of these parts is significant to fathoming how fiber optics capability and empower the transmission of information at the speed of light.

The glass center fills in as the focal channel for communicating light signals through the fiber optic link. Its determination is a basic part of the fiber optic plan, with glass being the transcendent material because of its straightforwardness and productive light transmission properties. The glass center is frequently produced using an extraordinary sort of glass with a high refractive list to work with all out interior reflection.

All out interior reflection is a principal optical peculiarity that happens while light going through a thick medium, like glass, experiences a limit with a less thick medium, similar to air or cladding, at a point more noteworthy than the basic point. With regards to fiber optics, this peculiarity guarantees that light remaining parts restricted to the glass center as it goes through numerous reflections, taking into consideration proficient transmission along the length of the fiber.

The plan of the glass center is a fastidious interaction that includes contemplations of aspects, immaculateness, and piece. The measurement of the center straightforwardly influences the exhibition of the fiber optic link. Single-mode strands, with a little center breadth, are intended for significant distance correspondence and high velocity information transmission. Conversely, multimode filaments, with a bigger center width, are reasonable for more limited distance correspondence inside structures or grounds.

The virtue of the glass is significant to limit signal misfortune during light transmission. Pollutants in the glass can assimilate or dissipate light, prompting constriction of the sign. Accordingly, makers cautiously control the piece of the glass to guarantee high straightforwardness and low sign misfortune, taking into account the successful transmission of information over significant distances.

Encompassing the glass center is the cladding, a layer of material with a lower refractive record than the center. The cladding assumes a urgent part in the all out interior reflection process, guaranteeing that light remaining parts kept to the center by bouncing off the center cladding limit. By keeping up with the basic plot for absolute inner reflection, the cladding forestalls signal spillage and misfortune.

The cladding material is commonly a sort of glass or plastic picked for its optical properties. It is painstakingly chosen to accomplish the ideal refractive record diverge from the center, establishing a climate helpful for absolute inner reflection. The elements of the cladding, like its thickness, are additionally basic in improving the optical execution of the fiber optic link.

The connection between the glass center and cladding is a fragile equilibrium. The refractive file of the cladding should be lower than that of the center to work with all out inward reflection, however it ought not be excessively low to stay away from extreme sign scattering. Appropriately planned cladding guarantees the effective engendering of light signals through the fiber optic link.

To safeguard the delicate glass center and cladding, a covering is applied to the outside of the fiber optic link. The covering fills various needs, including mechanical insurance, natural protection, and upgrade of generally speaking strength. It safeguards the fragile center and cladding from actual pressure, dampness, and other ecological variables that could think twice about trustworthiness of the fiber optic link.

The covering material is normally made of a polymer, like acrylate or polyimide, picked for its adaptability and defensive characteristics. The covering layer adds a degree of power to the fiber optic link, permitting it to endure bowing, winding, and different types of mechanical pressure. This is especially significant during establishment and sending, where links might be exposed to different outer powers.

Past mechanical security, the covering likewise fills in as a boundary against dampness and other ecological impurities. Openness to dampness can prompt sign debasement and compromise the exhibition of the fiber optic link. The covering goes about as a defensive safeguard, forestalling the entrance of dampness and guaranteeing the drawn out dependability of the link in different natural circumstances.

The decision of covering material and thickness is affected by variables like the expected application, establishment climate, and wanted adaptability of the fiber optic link. A few applications might require more slender and more adaptable coatings to work with simpler establishment and directing, while others might focus on thicker coatings for improved security in unforgiving conditions.

Notwithstanding its defensive capabilities, the covering likewise assumes a significant part in working with the taking care of and end of the fiber optic link. It gives a smooth external surface that considers simple joining, connectorization, and incorporation into different optical gadgets. The covering's similarity with industry-standard connectors guarantees interoperability and convenience in different optical correspondence frameworks.

The mix of the glass center, cladding, and covering makes a strong and effective construction for communicating light signals in fiber optic links. This painstakingly designed course of action use the standards of optics to empower high velocity information transmission over significant distances. The all out inside reflection inside the glass center, worked with by the cladding, guarantees that the light signals stay bound and travel along the length of the fiber with negligible sign misfortune.

The improvement of these center parts has gone through many years of exploration and refinement, bringing about an innovation that has become key to worldwide correspondence organizations. Fiber optics have altered broadcast communications as well as tracked down applications in different fields, including clinical imaging, detecting advancements, and modern cycles.

In clinical applications, fiber optics are essential to endoscopy, a negligibly obtrusive system that utilizes fiber optic groups to send light into the body and catch pictures for symptomatic purposes. The adaptability and little size of optical strands make them appropriate for exploring through the human body, giving doctors important visual data without the requirement for obtrusive medical procedure.

Fiber optic sensors, using the standards of light transmission and reflection, assume an essential part in enterprises like aviation, medical services, and natural checking. These sensors can recognize changes in temperature, tension, and strain by estimating varieties in light force or stage. The resistance of optical strands to electromagnetic obstruction makes them especially worthwhile in conditions where customary sensors might be defenseless to outer impacts.

The organization of fiber optic links has not just tended to the constraints of conventional copper-based correspondence frameworks however has additionally made the way for cutting edge innovations like frequency division multiplexing (WDM). WDM permits various frequencies of light to be sent at the same time through a solitary optical fiber, essentially expanding the general information limit and satisfying the raising need for higher information rates.

As the interest for higher transfer speed and quicker information transmission keeps on developing, specialists investigate new outskirts in fiber optic innovation. The improvement of empty central elements, with a center to some degree or completely made of air or another low-record material, addresses an inventive methodology. These strands offer special benefits, including lower signal scattering and the potential for communicating light in a more extensive scope of frequencies.

While fiber optic innovation has made astounding progress, continuous innovative work endeavors mean to address difficulties and push the limits of its abilities.

Signal constriction stays a thought, and scientists investigate ways of promoting limit misfortunes and upgrade signal respectability. Propels in assembling strategies keep on adding to cost decrease, making fiber optic organizations more available and boundless.

All in all, the center parts of fiber optics — the glass center, cladding, and covering — structure the underpinning of an extraordinary innovation that has reshaped the scene of correspondence and network. The careful plan and designing of these parts empower the effective transmission of information over significant distances with negligible sign misfortune. As fiber optic innovation keeps on developing, its effect reaches out past broadcast communications to a heap of utilizations that advantage from the novel properties and capacities of optical strands.

2.3 Role of light in data transmission

The job of light in information transmission is a urgent part of present day correspondence frameworks, assuming a focal part in the activity of advances like fiber optics. Light, as an electromagnetic wave, fills in as the transporter of data, considering fast and proficient transmission of information over significant distances. Understanding the standards of light in information transmission includes investigating ideas like balance, engendering, and the communication of light with materials inside optical frameworks.

At the center of light-based information transmission is the idea of tweak, where the qualities of a light wave are changed to encode data. Tweak considers the portrayal of double information, where varieties in the force, recurrence, or period of the light sign relate to the 0s and 1s of computerized data. This cycle is pivotal for changing over electrical signs, which are the normal language of electronic gadgets, into optical signs reasonable for transmission through fiber optic links.

Lasers and light-radiating diodes (LEDs) are the essential wellsprings of light utilized in information transmission frameworks. Lasers, with their sound and monochromatic properties, are especially appropriate for high velocity and significant distance correspondence. The utilization of lasers empowers exact command over the qualities of the light sign, taking into account effective adjustment and transmission of information. LEDs, albeit less rational than lasers, are broadly utilized in brief distance correspondence applications because of their expense adequacy and dependability.

The tweak cycle includes fluctuating at least one parts of the light sign to pass on data. Abundancy adjustment (AM), recurrence tweak (FM), and stage regulation (PM) are normal strategies utilized in optical correspondence frameworks. In adequacy balance, the power of the light wave is fluctuated to address paired information. Recurrence adjustment includes changing the recurrence of the light wave, while stage tweak modifies the period of the wave.

When the light sign is tweaked, it is sent into an optical medium, commonly an optical fiber on account of fiber optic correspondence. The properties of the optical medium assume a pivotal part in deciding the viability of light engendering. In optical strands, the center and cladding materials are painstakingly decided to work with complete interior reflection, permitting the light to be profoundly bound and engender over significant distances through various reflections.

The course of light proliferation in optical filaments is represented by Snell's Regulation, which portrays the connection between the point of occurrence and the point of refraction when light goes through various mediums. Complete interior reflection happens while light going through a denser medium, for example, the glass center of an optical fiber, experiences a limit with a less thick medium, similar to the cladding, at a point more noteworthy than the basic point. This peculiarity guarantees that the light remaining parts inside the center, forestalling signal misfortune and empowering productive information transmission.

The capacity of light to go through optical strands with insignificant sign misfortune is a critical benefit of fiber optic correspondence over customary copper-based frameworks. Copper links experience the ill effects of sign corruption over distance because of opposition and different variables, while optical filaments experience altogether lower weakening, considering information transmission over a lot more noteworthy distances without the requirement for continuous sign intensification.

As light proliferates through the optical fiber, it might experience scattering, a peculiarity where various frequencies of light travel at various velocities. Chromatic scattering and modular scattering are two sorts of scattering that can affect the nature of information transmission. Chromatic scattering results from varieties in the speed of light with various frequencies, causing various tones (or frequencies) of light to fan out over distance. Modular scattering, then again, happens in multimode filaments because of varieties in the ways that various methods of light can take.

To alleviate the impacts of scattering, different scattering the board strategies are utilized. At times, various kinds of strands, like single-mode filaments with a little center breadth, are utilized to decrease scattering. Furthermore, the utilization of frequency division multiplexing (WDM), where numerous frequencies of light are sent all the while through a solitary optical fiber, can help make up for scattering impacts by taking into consideration more exact command over the various frequencies.

The regulation, proliferation, and scattering the executives angles on the whole add to the effectiveness and dependability of light-based information transmission in optical correspondence frameworks. The standards administering these cycles are fundamental for the plan and activity of fiber optic organizations that structure the foundation of current media communications.

The qualities of light, for example, its speed and capacity to convey data as adjusted signals, make it an optimal mechanism for information transmission. The speed of light in a vacuum is roughly 299,792 kilometers each second (186,282 miles each second), and albeit light ventures somewhat more slow in optical filaments because of the refractive record of the materials, it actually considers very quick information transmission contrasted with conventional copper-based frameworks.

The upsides of light-based information transmission stretch out past speed and productivity. One critical advantage is the resistance of optical filaments to electromagnetic impedance. Not at all like copper links, which can be vulnerable to outer electromagnetic impacts, optical strands are not impacted by such impedance. This resistance makes fiber optic correspondence frameworks profoundly solid and reasonable for conditions where electromagnetic impedance is a worry.

One more benefit of light-based information transmission is the potential for high data transfer capacity. The utilization of different frequencies in WDM innovation empowers the synchronous transmission of numerous information streams over a solitary optical fiber. Every frequency fills in as a free channel, actually expanding the general information limit of the fiber. This capacity to deal with high transfer speed is vital in satisfying the developing need for quicker information rates in present day correspondence organizations.

The organization of fiber optic links has changed different parts of correspondence, including web availability, phone organizations, and satellite TV. The high transfer speed, low sign misfortune, and significant distance transmission abilities of fiber optics pursue it an optimal decision for these applications. The unwavering quality and productivity of optical strands have additionally added to the expansion of rapid internet providers and the consistent exchange of tremendous measures of information around the world.

Past broadcast communications, the job of light in information transmission stretches out to applications in clinical imaging, detecting advances, and modern cycles. In clinical endoscopy, for instance, fiber optic groups send light into the body to catch pictures for demonstrative purposes. The adaptability and little size of optical filaments make them appropriate for exploring through the human body, giving doctors significant visual data without the requirement for intrusive medical procedure.

Fiber optic sensors influence the standards of light transmission and reflection to identify changes in temperature, tension, or strain. These sensors are utilized in different enterprises, including aviation, medical services, and natural observing. The capacity to send information involving light makes optical strands ideal for applications where customary sensors might be unrealistic or helpless to outer impacts.

The job of light in information transmission likewise reaches out to trend setting innovations like quantum correspondence. Quantum optics standards are applied to control and send data utilizing individual photons. Quantum correspondence utilizing fiber optics holds the commitment of super secure correspondence channels, as any endeavor to block the quantum condition of a photon would be distinguishable.

Notwithstanding the spread of light inside optical strands, the cooperation of light with materials inside the optical framework is a basic thought. The selection of materials for the center, cladding, and covering of the optical fiber impacts the effectiveness of light transmission and the general presentation of the correspondence framework.

The center material, normally made of glass, is picked for its straightforwardness and capacity to communicate light effectively. The immaculateness of the glass is vital to limit signal misfortune, as pollutants can retain or disperse light. The refractive file of the center material is painstakingly chosen to work with complete inward reflection and guarantee the imprisonment of light inside the center.

The cladding material, encompassing the center, has a lower refractive record to empower complete interior reflection and forestall signal spillage. The aspects and piece of the cladding are basic in keeping up with the optical properties of the fiber. Appropriately planned cladding guarantees the proficient proliferation of light signals through the fiber optic link.

To safeguard the delicate center and cladding, a covering is applied to the outside of the fiber optic link. The covering material, ordinarily a polymer, gives mechanical insurance, ecological protection, and in general toughness. The covering safeguards the optical fiber from actual pressure, dampness, and other ecological elements that could think twice about trustworthiness.

The decision of covering material and thickness relies upon elements like the expected application, establishment climate, and wanted adaptability of the fiber optic link. More slender and more adaptable coatings might be utilized for applications where simple establishment and directing are fundamental, while thicker coatings give upgraded security in brutal conditions.

The standards of light-based information transmission, enveloping adjustment, engendering, and the collaboration of light with materials, have made ready for the improvement of advances that structure the foundation of present day correspondence frameworks. Fiber optics, with their capacity to send information at the speed of light over significant distances, have reformed how data is conveyed, associating individuals and empowering the consistent trade of information around the world.

The continuous advancement of light-based information transmission includes consistent innovative work endeavors to upgrade the proficiency, dependability, and abilities of optical correspondence frameworks.

As the interest for higher transfer speed, quicker information rates, and secure correspondence channels develops, analysts investigate new boondocks, including quantum correspondence and high level materials for optical parts.

2.4 Advantages of fiber optics over traditional copper cables

The upsides of fiber optics over conventional copper links address a huge jump forward in the field of correspondence and information transmission. Fiber optic innovation outfits the properties of light to communicate information, offering a few key advantages that put it aside from regular copper-based frameworks. Understanding these benefits requires an investigation of elements like transmission capacity, signal honesty, speed, and protection from outer impacts.

One of the essential benefits of fiber optics is the considerably higher transmission capacity they give contrasted with conventional copper links. Transfer speed alludes to the limit of a correspondence channel to communicate information. Fiber optic links can uphold a lot more noteworthy transfer speeds than copper links, considering the concurrent transmission of a lot of information over various channels. This expanded transfer speed is especially critical in the period of top quality video web based, distributed computing, and different information concentrated applications.

The high transmission capacity of fiber optics is intently attached to their capacity to help many frequencies and frequencies. This adaptability empowers the utilization of cutting edge innovations, for example, frequency division multiplexing (WDM). WDM permits various frequencies of light, each conveying its own information stream, to be sent at the same time over a solitary optical fiber. This capacity decisively builds the general information limit of the fiber, giving a versatile answer for satisfy developing needs for higher information rates.

Notwithstanding higher data transmission, fiber optics display altogether lower signal misfortune over significant distances contrasted with copper links. Copper links experience the ill effects of sign corruption because of opposition, particularly as the distance between the transmitter and recipient increments. Conversely, optical filaments experience negligible sign misfortune, taking into consideration information transmission over a lot more noteworthy distances without the requirement for incessant sign intensification. This trademark makes fiber optics ideal for long stretch correspondence joins and undersea links.

The low sign misfortune in fiber optics is a consequence of the rule of complete interior reflection. As light goes through the glass center of an optical fiber, it goes through numerous reflections, guaranteeing that the sign remaining parts kept profoundly. This peculiarity limits the weakening of the light sign, saving its respectability overstretched distances. Conversely, copper links experience the ill effects of sign corruption because of variables like obstruction and electromagnetic impedance, requiring the utilization of repeaters to help the sign.

The proficiency of light engendering in optical strands adds to their capacity to send information at a lot higher velocities than copper links. The speed of information transmission in fiber optics is regularly estimated as far as the speed of light in the medium, which is roughly 200,000 kilometers each second (124,274 miles each second) in optical strands. This fast transmission is fundamental for satisfying the needs of utilizations requiring quick information move, for example, ongoing video web based, internet gaming, and high-recurrence monetary exchanges.

The speed of light in optical filaments is a consequence of the low refractive record of the center material, which works with fast light engendering. In copper links, electrical signs travel for a portion of the speed of light, and sign corruption over distance requires the utilization of sign repeaters. The innate speed of light in fiber optics, combined with low sign misfortune, adds to the prevalent presentation of optical correspondence frameworks.

One more striking benefit of fiber optics is their protection from electromagnetic obstruction (EMI) and radio-recurrence impedance (RFI). Copper links, being electrical channels, are defenseless to obstruction from outside electromagnetic sources. This obstruction can prompt sign corruption, influencing the nature of information transmission. Fiber optic links, then again, send information utilizing light signals, which are resistant to EMI and RFI. This obstruction makes fiber optics especially reasonable for conditions where electromagnetic impedance is a worry, like modern settings or regions with high radio-recurrence action.

The insusceptibility of fiber optics to electromagnetic impedance is a consequence of the actual properties of light and the way that optical strands don't direct power. This trademark makes fiber optic correspondence frameworks profoundly dependable in circumstances where conventional copper links might encounter disturbances because of outer impacts. It likewise takes into consideration the conjunction of fiber optic links with other electronic hardware unafraid of obstruction.

As far as actual qualities, fiber optics offer an extensive benefit regarding size and weight. Optical filaments are a lot more slender and lighter than copper links, making them more adaptable and simpler to introduce. The diminished size and weight of fiber optic links are especially worthwhile in applications where space imperatives or weight contemplations are basic, like in airplane, submarines, or thickly populated metropolitan regions.

The actual qualities of fiber optics likewise add to their solidness and protection from ecological variables. Optical strands are less helpless to consumption and don't confront similar difficulties as copper links, which can erode over the long run. Moreover, the defensive covering on fiber optic links safeguards them from dampness and other ecological components, guaranteeing their life span and unwavering quality in different circumstances.

The solidness of fiber optics stretches out to their protection from temperature changes, making them appropriate for organization in outrageous conditions. Optical filaments can endure a more extensive scope of temperatures contrasted with copper links, making them ideal for applications in businesses like aviation, where temperature varieties are normal. This strength adds to the general dependability and soundness of fiber optic correspondence frameworks.

Fiber optics likewise offer improved security concerning information transmission. Dissimilar to copper links, which produce electromagnetic signs that can be captured and taken advantage of, fiber optic links don't emanate signals. The transmission of light through optical filaments is deeply bound, making it hard for outer substances to capture or listen in on the information being sent. This inborn security highlight goes with fiber optics a favored decision for applications where information secrecy is principal.

The security of fiber optic correspondence is additionally increased by the utilization of cutting edge encryption procedures. As information goes as adjusted light signals, encryption strategies can be applied to get the data being communicated. This layered way to deal with security guarantees that regardless of whether somebody were to take advantage of the fiber optic link, the captured information would remain encoded and unintelligible.

The upsides of fiber optics over customary copper links stretch out to their expense viability over the long haul. While the underlying organization cost of fiber optic foundation might be higher than that of copper-based frameworks, the complete expense of responsibility for life cycle is many times lower. The sturdiness, life span, and low upkeep necessities of fiber optic links add to cost reserve funds over the long run. Furthermore, the capacity to send more information over longer distances without the requirement for signal repeaters diminishes functional expenses and gives a versatile answer for future development.

All in all, the upsides of fiber optics over conventional copper links envelop a great many variables, including higher data transfer capacity, lower signal misfortune, sped up, protection from electromagnetic obstruction, actual qualities, security, and cost-viability. The change from copper-based correspondence frameworks to fiber optics has been a groundbreaking jump in the field of media communications and information transmission. The predominant presentation and dependability of fiber optics make them an imperative innovation that supports the computerized network of the cutting edge world. As the interest for higher information rates, more prominent transmission capacity, and secure correspondence channels keeps on developing, fiber optics stand as a foundation innovation that will assume a focal part in molding the eventual fate of worldwide correspondence organizations.

Chapter 3

Building the Fiber Backbone

Building the fiber spine of an advanced correspondence network is a mind boggling and multi-layered try that requires fastidious preparation, critical assets, and state of the art innovation. This central framework shapes the reason for high velocity web availability, empowering consistent correspondence and information move across tremendous distances. As the interest for quicker and more dependable internet providers keeps on developing, the significance of a strong fiber spine couldn't possibly be more significant.

The most vital phase in building a fiber spine includes exhaustive preparation and practicality studies. Specialists and organizers should evaluate the geological and geographical elements of the area to decide the ideal courses for laying fiber optic links. Factors like territory, populace thickness, existing foundation, and potential deterrents should be considered to make a well defined plan that limits costs and boosts effectiveness.

When the arranging stage is finished, the real organization of the fiber optic organization can start. This interaction includes the establishment of fiber optic links along the foreordained courses. The links are commonly covered underground or introduced on utility shafts, contingent upon the particular prerequisites of the undertaking. The establishment cycle is multifaceted, requiring specific gear and gifted professionals to guarantee the legitimate arrangement and association of the fiber optic links.

One of the basic contemplations in building a fiber spine is the determination of the right kind of fiber optic link. Single-mode and multi-mode strands are the two essential classifications, each with its novel qualities. Single-mode strands are intended for significant distance transmission with a solitary light mode, while multi-mode filaments can convey numerous light modes over more limited distances. The decision between these choices relies upon the organization's planned use and the distance the signs need to travel.

Notwithstanding the sort of fiber optic link, the choice of systems administration gear is similarly critical. Optical handsets, switches, and switches assume a crucial part in the general presentation and dependability of the fiber spine. These parts should be painstakingly decided to guarantee similarity and ideal usefulness. As innovation develops, network organizers should keep up to date with the furthest down the line headways to settle on informed choices that improve the organization's capacities.

As the actual framework comes to fruition, consideration goes to the execution of availability arrangements. Fiber optic joining and end are fundamental cycles that guarantee the consistent association of links and keep up with signal trustworthiness. Accuracy is fundamental in these systems, as any deviation can bring about signal misfortune and compromise the organization's presentation. High level apparatuses and hardware are utilized to accomplish the important accuracy in joining and end.

The fruitful organization of a fiber spine likewise depends on compelling task the board. Timetables, financial plans, and assets should be painstakingly figured out how to keep away from deferrals and cost invades. Unanticipated difficulties, like harsh weather conditions or surprising hindrances during establishment, require versatile venture the board methodologies. Steady correspondence and coordination among the undertaking colleagues are fundamental for address issues speedily and keep the venture on target.

Besides, administrative consistence is a critical part of building a fiber spine. Nearby, provincial, and public guidelines should be explored to acquire the essential licenses and endorsements for the organization sending. Ecological effect appraisals and adherence to somewhere safe and secure principles are indispensable to guaranteeing the venture lines up with legitimate and moral rules. Joint effort with administrative bodies and partners is imperative to streamline possible obstacles and smooth out the endorsement cycle.

As the actual framework approaches fruition, testing turns into a basic stage in the sending of a fiber spine. Thorough testing techniques are carried out to confirm the respectability and execution of the organization. Optical time-space reflectometers (OTDRs) are regularly used to recognize and find any shortcomings or anomalies in the fiber optic links. Moreover, power misfortune estimations and sign quality evaluations are directed to guarantee that the organization meets the predefined execution measures.

With the fiber spine set up, the center movements to organize streamlining and support. Progressing observing and preventive upkeep are fundamental to distinguish and resolve expected issues before they raise. Network the executives frameworks are utilized to remotely screen the wellbeing and execution of the foundation, taking into account proactive mediation and limiting personal time.

Versatility is one more significant thought in building a fiber spine. As the interest for transmission capacity expands, the organization should be fit for obliging higher information volumes without compromising execution. Future-sealing the framework requires vital preparation and the fuse of innovations that help adaptability, for example, frequency division multiplexing (WDM) and high level adjustment procedures.

The organization of a fiber spine likewise opens up open doors for the execution of arising innovations. The coming of 5G network, the Web of Things (IoT), and shrewd city drives further highlight the significance of a strong fiber foundation. The low inertness and high transmission capacity given by fiber optics act as the establishment for these extraordinary advancements, empowering another period of availability and development.

Notwithstanding mechanical contemplations, constructing a fiber spine includes tending to financial and social variables. The monetary practicality of the task is affected by variables like profit from speculation (return on initial capital investment), money saving advantage examination, and potential income streams. Social contemplations incorporate guaranteeing impartial admittance to rapid web in both metropolitan and provincial regions, crossing over the computerized separation, and encouraging inclusivity.

Public-private organizations frequently assume an essential part in the improvement of fiber spine framework. Joint effort between government substances, broadcast communications organizations, and different partners can use assets and aptitude, facilitating the arrangement interaction. These organizations can likewise work with the sharing of framework, diminishing expenses and limiting duplication of endeavors.

Security is a fundamental worry in any correspondence organization, and the fiber spine is no special case. Executing hearty online protection measures is basic to shield the respectability and privacy of information communicated over the organization. Encryption, firewalls, and interruption recognition frameworks are fundamental parts of a complete security system. Normal security reviews and updates are directed to remain in front of developing digital dangers.

The advantages of a deep rooted fiber spine reach out past rapid web access. Further developed availability upgrades instructive open doors, upholds telemedicine drives, and animates monetary turn of events. Organizations can use the framework for additional effective tasks, and people can appreciate upgraded amusement and correspondence encounters. The cultural effect of a powerful fiber spine is broad, adding to the general prosperity and progress of networks.

As the computerized scene keeps on advancing, the job of the fiber spine in molding the eventual fate of correspondence couldn't possibly be more significant. The continuous improvement of new innovations, for example, quantum correspondence and cutting edge organizing principles, highlights the requirement for an adaptable and versatile fiber foundation. The consistent development of the fiber spine is a demonstration of the unique idea of the media communications industry.

All in all, constructing the fiber spine of a cutting edge correspondence network is a diverse and dynamic cycle that requires cautious preparation, cutting edge innovation, and joint effort among different partners. From the underlying preparation and possibility studies to the continuous enhancement and upkeep, each stage assumes a pivotal part in guaranteeing the outcome of the framework. The sending of a strong fiber spine not just addresses the ongoing interest for rapid web yet in addition makes way for future developments and groundbreaking advancements. As the computerized time keeps on unfurling, the significance of a dependable and versatile fiber spine will stay at the very front of worldwide network and correspondence.

3.1 Deployment of fiber optic infrastructure on a large scale

The sending of fiber optic framework for an enormous scope is a key and multifaceted interaction that includes fastidious preparation, exact execution, and coordination across different spaces. As the interest for fast web keeps on flooding, the sending of fiber optics has become progressively vital in gathering the developing necessities of organizations, families, and foundations. This exhaustive endeavor includes a few key stages, each adding to the foundation of a powerful and solid fiber optic organization.

The underlying phase of enormous scope fiber optic sending includes a careful evaluation of the geological and geographical highlights of the objective region. Designers and organizers lead plausibility studies to recognize ideal courses for laying fiber optic links. Factors like territory, populace thickness, existing framework, and potential snags are painstakingly considered to make a masterful arrangement that limits costs and boosts the productivity of the sending.

When the arranging stage is finished, the real organization of fiber optic links starts. This cycle requires specific gear, talented experts, and adherence to severe quality guidelines. The establishment techniques shift contingent upon the particular necessities of the venture. Fiber optic links are regularly covered underground or introduced on utility shafts. The decision between these strategies is affected by variables like metropolitan thickness, natural contemplations, and the need to limit disturbance to existing framework.

The determination of the right kind of fiber optic link is a basic choice in the organization cycle. Single-mode and multi-mode filaments are the two essential classes, each intended for explicit use cases. Single-mode filaments are reasonable for significant distance transmission with a solitary light mode, while multi-mode strands are utilized for more limited removes and can convey various light modes at the same time. The decision between these choices relies upon the organization's expected use and the distances signals need to cross.

As well as choosing the proper sort of fiber optic link, the sending group should cautiously pick organizing gear to guarantee similarity and ideal usefulness. Optical handsets, switches, and switches are vital parts of the fiber optic organization. Keeping up to date with innovative progressions is fundamental for pursue informed choices that improve the organization's abilities and life span.

Fiber optic joining and end are basic cycles that guarantee the consistent association of links and keep up with signal honesty. Accuracy is fundamental in these methods, as any deviation can bring about signal misfortune and compromise the organization's presentation. High level apparatuses and hardware, like combination splicers, are utilized to accomplish the essential accuracy in joining and end.

Compelling venture the executives is fundamental for the progress of enormous scope fiber optic sending. Timetables, financial plans, and assets should be painstakingly figured out how to keep away from deferrals and cost overwhelms. Unanticipated difficulties, like nasty weather conditions or unforeseen snags during establishment, require versatile task the board techniques. Steady correspondence and coordination among colleagues are fundamental for address issues quickly and keep the undertaking on target.

Administrative consistence is a critical part of huge scope fiber optic sending. Neighborhood, provincial, and public guidelines should be explored to get the important grants and endorsements for the organization sending. Ecological effect evaluations and adherence to somewhere safe and secure norms are basic to guaranteeing the venture lines up with lawful and moral rules. Coordinated effort with administrative bodies and partners is essential to streamline expected jumps and smooth out the endorsement cycle.

As the actual framework comes to fruition, thorough testing turns into a critical stage in the organization cycle. Different testing techniques are executed to check the uprightness and execution of the organization. Optical time-space reflectometers (OTDRs) are regularly used to recognize and find any issues or anomalies in the fiber optic links. Also, power misfortune estimations and sign quality appraisals are led to guarantee that the organization meets the predetermined presentation rules.

With the fiber optic framework set up, the center movements to arrange enhancement and support. Continuous checking and preventive upkeep are fundamental to distinguish and resolve expected issues before they raise. Network the board frameworks are utilized to remotely screen the wellbeing and execution of the foundation, taking into account proactive mediation and limiting personal time.

Adaptability is one more basic thought in enormous scope fiber optic organization. The organization should be intended to oblige future development and expanded interest for data transmission without compromising execution. Future-sealing the foundation requires vital preparation and the fuse of innovations that help versatility, for example, frequency division multiplexing (WDM) and high level balance methods.

Enormous scope fiber optic organization additionally opens up open doors for the execution of arising advancements. The coming of 5G network, the Web of Things (IoT), and shrewd city drives further highlight the significance of a powerful fiber framework.

The low dormancy and high transmission capacity given by fiber optics act as the establishment for these extraordinary advancements, empowering another period of availability and development.

Additionally, the financial and social effect of enormous scope fiber optic sending can't be ignored. The monetary reasonability of the undertaking is affected by variables like profit from speculation (return for money invested), money saving advantage investigation, and potential income streams. Social contemplations incorporate guaranteeing fair admittance to high velocity web in both metropolitan and provincial regions, connecting the computerized gap, and encouraging inclusivity.

Public-private organizations frequently assume a urgent part in the sending of fiber optic framework for an enormous scope. Coordinated effort between government elements, broadcast communications organizations, and different partners can use assets and aptitude, assisting the arrangement cycle. These associations can likewise work with the sharing of framework, diminishing expenses and limiting duplication of endeavors.

Security is a fundamental worry in any correspondence organization, and enormous scope fiber optic sending is no exemption. Carrying out hearty online protection measures is basic to defend the trustworthiness and privacy of information communicated over the organization. Encryption, firewalls, and interruption discovery frameworks are fundamental parts of an extensive security methodology. Customary security reviews and updates are led to remain in front of developing digital dangers.

The advantages of enormous scope fiber optic sending stretch out past fast web access. Further developed network improves instructive open doors, upholds telemedicine drives, and animates monetary turn of events. Organizations can use the framework for additional productive tasks, and people can appreciate improved diversion and correspondence encounters. The cultural effect of huge scope fiber optic organization is extensive, adding to the general prosperity and progress of networks.

As the computerized scene keeps on advancing, the job of fiber optic framework in molding the fate of correspondence is unquestionable. The continuous improvement of new innovations, for example, quantum correspondence and cutting edge organizing principles, highlights the requirement for an adaptable and versatile fiber foundation. The ceaseless development of huge scope fiber optic organization is a demonstration of the unique idea of the media communications industry.

All in all, the organization of fiber optic framework for an enormous scope is a perplexing and multi-layered process that requires cautious preparation, cutting edge innovation, and cooperation among different partners.

From the underlying preparation and possibility studies to the continuous enhancement and support, each stage assumes a significant part in guaranteeing the progress of the sending. The foundation of a hearty fiber optic organization not just addresses the ongoing interest for rapid web yet additionally makes way for future developments and groundbreaking innovations. As the computerized period keeps on unfurling, the significance of a solid and versatile fiber optic foundation will stay at the very front of worldwide network and correspondence.

3.2 Challenges and solutions in laying fiber optic cables

Laying fiber optic links presents a large group of difficulties that require cautious thought and inventive answers for guarantee the fruitful organization of strong and solid correspondence organizations. As interest for rapid web keeps on heightening, tending to these difficulties becomes fundamental in gathering the developing availability needs of organizations, families, and establishments. This conversation investigates the different difficulties experienced in laying fiber optic links and the relating arrangements that industry experts utilize to conquer them.

One huge test in laying fiber optic links is the mind boggling arranging expected to explore complex metropolitan conditions. Urban communities are described by thickly pressed framework, including utilities, streets, and existing media transmission organizations. Organizing with nearby specialists, metropolitan organizers, and service organizations is fundamental to distinguish ideal courses that limit interruption and keep away from clashes with existing foundation. High level planning and looking over advances assume an essential part in this stage, giving precise information to design effective courses and address likely snags.

Also, the establishment of fiber optic links in metropolitan regions frequently includes managing blocked underground spaces. Getting to utility passageways and exploring around existing lines and links requires particular hardware and talented experts. Level directional boring (HDD) and microtrenching are procedures utilized to limit the interruption brought about by conventional digging strategies. These methodologies consider the establishment of fiber optic links underneath existing framework, decreasing the requirement for broad unearthing and limiting effect on everyday metropolitan exercises.

Notwithstanding metropolitan difficulties, laying fiber optic links in country or distant regions presents its own arrangement of snags. The immense spreads and testing territories normal for provincial scenes can entangle the sending system. Restricted framework, unforgiving atmospheric conditions, and the shortfall of promptly accessible assets present difficulties that request inventive arrangements. Conveying airborne fiber optic links on utility shafts or using particular hardware for digging in provincial conditions can assist with conquering these moves and stretch out fast network to underserved regions.

One more basic test in laying fiber optic links is the requirement for significant monetary ventures. The expense of materials, gear, work, and allows can add to a critical monetary weight.

Also, unanticipated difficulties during sending can prompt expense overwhelms. To address these monetary difficulties, key preparation and a complete money saving advantage investigation are fundamental. Public-private organizations can likewise assume a urgent part, with government elements teaming up with private broadcast communications organizations to share expenses and assets. This cooperative methodology helps make huge scope fiber optic arrangement financially reasonable and speeds up the development of high velocity availability.

Natural contemplations are indispensable to fiber optic link arrangement and posture difficulties connected with environmental effect and maintainability. Conventional digging strategies can upset biological systems, upset untamed life natural surroundings, and add to soil disintegration. To alleviate these natural worries, industry experts progressively take on eco-accommodating establishment strategies. Even directional penetrating and microtrenching, referenced prior, are techniques that diminish the environmental impression of arrangement. Moreover, adherence to ecological guidelines and the execution of best practices in natural surroundings protection add to earth capable fiber optic link establishment.

Specialized difficulties in laying fiber optic links incorporate guaranteeing signal honesty and limiting sign constriction. As information goes over significant distances through fiber optic links, signal misfortune can happen because of elements like bowing, joining, and ecological circumstances. To address this test, exact establishment methods and top notch materials are fundamental. Standard testing, utilizing devices like optical time-space reflectometers (OTDRs), distinguishes and find any sign misfortune or anomalies in the fiber optic links. The utilization of cutting edge fiber optic connectors and joining advances further improves signal uprightness and limits execution corruption.

One of the determined difficulties in fiber optic link arrangement is the gamble of harm during development or upkeep exercises. Removal work, unintentional cuts, or development related occurrences can prompt link harm, disturbing correspondence administrations.

Executing vigorous defensive measures, for example, covering links at adequate profundities or introducing defensive channels, mitigates the gamble of unplanned harm. Also, carrying out far reaching wellbeing preparing for development groups and consolidating harm counteraction conventions are pivotal parts of hazard the board in fiber optic organization projects.

Fiber optic links are defenseless to natural factors like temperature varieties, dampness, and outrageous atmospheric conditions. These variables can affect the links' presentation and life span. Utilizing links with climate safe coatings and carrying out appropriate establishment methods, for example, fixing link joints, safeguards against ecological difficulties. Progressing checking and upkeep are likewise fundamental to recognize and resolve potential issues instantly, guaranteeing the drawn out unwavering quality of the fiber optic organization.

Administrative difficulties can present huge obstacles in the sending of fiber optic links. Getting grants and endorsements from neighborhood, territorial, and public specialists is a tedious cycle that can prompt venture delays. Smoothing out administrative cycles and encouraging cooperation between broadcast communications organizations and administrative bodies are fundamental for speeding up the endorsement stage. Drawing in with nearby networks and tending to their interests through straightforward correspondence can assist with building support for fiber optic sending projects and work with smoother administrative cycles.

As the broadcast communications industry develops, the test of staying up with innovative headways remains ever-present. Arising innovations, like 5G availability and quantum correspondence, request foundation that upholds higher data transmissions and low-inactivity correspondence. Future-sealing fiber optic organizations requires consistent innovative work to consolidate the most recent mechanical advancements. Overhauling hardware and taking on adaptable designs, for example, those empowered by programming characterized organizing (SDN) and network capability virtualization (NFV), guarantees that fiber optic organizations stay at the cutting edge of mechanical advancement.

All in all, laying fiber optic links for a huge scope includes exploring a horde of difficulties, going from metropolitan arranging intricacies and monetary contemplations to specialized and natural obstructions. The answers for these difficulties require a multi-layered approach that coordinates cutting edge innovations, inventive organization strategies, and joint effort among partners. Key preparation, natural obligation, adherence to guidelines, and progressing support are urgent components in defeating the difficulties related with fiber optic link organization. As the interest for high velocity web keeps on rising, tending to these difficulties becomes basic for guaranteeing the consistent development of solid and productive correspondence organizations. The proceeded with advancement of fiber optic sending rehearses is critical in forming the eventual fate of worldwide network and correspondence.

3.3 Importance of a robust backbone for high-speed internet

The significance of a strong spine for fast web couldn't possibly be more significant in our undeniably associated and computerized world. A vigorous spine fills in as the groundwork of the whole web foundation, empowering the consistent and effective exchange of information across tremendous distances. As the interest for quicker and more dependable internet providers keeps on developing, the meaning of areas of strength for a versatile spine turns out to be much more basic.

At its center, the foundation of the web is an organization of high-limit, significant distance correspondence interfaces that interface different marks of presence (POPs) all over the planet. These connections structure the framework that conveys the main part of web traffic, working with correspondence between various organizations, web access suppliers (ISPs), and end-clients. The spine basically goes about as the focal sensory system of the web, giving the essential foundation to the trading of information at fantastic velocities.

One of the essential explanations behind the significance of a powerful spine is the rising interest for rapid internet providers. With the expansion of transfer speed concentrated applications, like real time top quality video, internet gaming, and cloud-based administrations, there is a developing requirement for networks that can deal with enormous volumes of information with low idleness. A strong spine guarantees that the web can uphold these transfer speed escalated applications, furnishing clients with a consistent and responsive internet based insight.

Besides, the spine assumes a urgent part in associating various locales and nations, working with worldwide correspondence and coordinated effort. Organizations, instructive foundations, and people depend on high velocity web for exercises, for example, video conferencing, document sharing, and continuous information move. A vigorous spine guarantees that information can traverse mainlands rapidly and effectively, encouraging worldwide network and empowering a really interconnected world.

The spine additionally fills in as the foundation that supports arising advancements, like the Web of Things (IoT) and 5G availability. These advances depend on low-inactivity and high-data transfer capacity organizations to successfully work. The spine, with its rapid connections and progressed organizing gear, gives the fundamental framework to the broad reception of these extraordinary innovations. As IoT gadgets become more predominant and 5G organizations carry out, the interest for a vigorous spine will just keep on expanding.

The dependability and strength of the web spine are urgent for guaranteeing ceaseless and continuous availability. Personal time or disturbances in the spine can have far and wide outcomes, influencing organizations, crisis administrations, and regular exercises that depend on web availability. Overt repetitiveness and failover systems are coordinated into the spine framework to limit the effect of likely disappointments and guarantee that information can stream flawlessly even notwithstanding network disturbances.

Notwithstanding its job in supporting fast web access for end-clients, the spine is instrumental in working with the productive trade of information between various organizations and ISPs. This cycle, known as looking, permits organizations to interconnect and share traffic straightforwardly, lessening the dependence on outsider mediators. Looking arrangements between networks add to the general effectiveness of the web, empowering information to take the most immediate and productive course between its source and objective.

The spine likewise assumes an imperative part in supporting the development of computerized economies. As organizations progressively depend on internet based stages for business, correspondence, and cooperation, a powerful spine becomes fundamental for working with internet business exchanges, internet banking, and computerized administrations. The capacity to send enormous volumes of information rapidly and safely is basic to the progress of computerized organizations and the more extensive advanced economy.

Moreover, the foundation of the web is fundamental to supporting progressions in fields like medical care, training, and examination. Telemedicine, online training, and cooperative exploration projects rely upon high velocity web availability to successfully work. A vigorous spine guarantees that these basic administrations can work flawlessly, paying little mind to geological distances, empowering admittance to data and mastery on a worldwide scale.

The development of the spine framework is intently attached to headways in fiber optic innovation. Fiber optic links, which use beats of light to communicate information, offer altogether higher data transmission and lower dormancy contrasted with customary copper links. The organization of fiber optic links in the spine improves the general limit of the web and supports the interest for higher information move rates. Nonstop interests in overhauling and growing fiber optic organizations are vital for keeping a powerful spine that can meet the developing requirements of clients and applications.

Security is one more foremost thought with regards to the web spine. As information traversed the spine, it is fundamental for carry out strong safety efforts to safeguard against digital dangers and guarantee the classification and respectability of sent data. Encryption, firewalls, interruption location frameworks, and other security conventions are carried out to shield the spine foundation. Given the rising complexity of digital dangers, continuous endeavors to upgrade the security of the web spine are basic.

The significance of a hearty spine reaches out to the idea of internet fairness — a rule that promoters for equivalent and unprejudiced treatment of all web traffic. An unbiased and open spine guarantees that information is communicated without separation, no matter what its source, objective, or content. This rule is primary to keeping a level battleground on the web, cultivating development, contest, and free articulation. A strong spine that maintains the standards of internet fairness is fundamental for protecting the majority rule nature of the web.

The worldwide idea of the web requires global coordinated effort in keeping up with and growing the spine framework. Coordination between various districts, nations, and organization administrators is fundamental for guaranteeing the consistent progression of information across borders. Worldwide principles and arrangements assume a part in fitting the turn of events and upkeep of spine framework on a worldwide scale. Furthermore, cooperative endeavors in innovative work add to the nonstop improvement of spine advancements.

As the interest for high velocity web keeps on developing, the eventual fate of the spine will be molded by continuous mechanical headways and advancements. The sending of cutting edge advancements, like 6G network, quantum correspondence, and edge figuring, will put new expectations on the spine foundation. Adjusting to these mechanical movements requires a guarantee to innovative work, interest in state of the art innovations, and a proactive way to deal with tending to arising difficulties.

All in all, the significance of a powerful spine for rapid web couldn't possibly be more significant in our interconnected and computerized world. The spine fills in as the focal foundation that supports the whole web, empowering the consistent exchange of information across the globe. Its part in supporting high velocity network, working with worldwide correspondence, and supporting arising innovations makes it a foundation of our cutting edge computerized society. As the web keeps on advancing, the continuous turn of events and support of a strong spine will stay significant for satisfying the developing needs of clients, organizations, and the more extensive computerized economy.

3.4 Real-world examples of successful fiber optic networks

The fruitful organization and activity of fiber optic organizations have changed the manner in which we associate, impart, and access data. Certifiable instances of these organizations grandstand their effect on different areas, from media communications and internet providers to medical care, schooling, and then some. Analyzing these examples of overcoming adversity gives experiences into the potential and adaptability of fiber optic organizations in tending to different availability needs.

Google Fiber (US):

Google Fiber is a high velocity fiber optic web access given by Letters in order Inc., Google's parent organization. Sent off at first in Kansas City in 2012, Google Fiber has extended to a few urban communities across the US. It offers gigabit-speed web access, furnishing clients with outstandingly quick download and transfer speeds. The outcome of Google Fiber lies in its speed as well as in its obligation to reasonableness and client support. The drive has prodded rivalry in the broadband market, empowering other specialist organizations to upgrade their organizations and deal higher-speed choices.

Singapore's Cross country Broadband Organization (NBN):

Singapore's NBN is an administration driven drive pointed toward giving rapid broadband admittance to occupants and organizations across the island country. Sent in numerous stages, the NBN use fiber optic innovation to convey super quick web network. The organization incorporates both private and business associations, supporting many administrations, including working from home, e-learning, and shrewd city applications. Singapore's obligation to building a strong fiber optic organization has added to its status as one of the most associated and carefully progressed countries universally.

Japan's Web Drive Japan (IIJ):

Web Drive Japan (IIJ) is a Japanese web access supplier that plays had a critical impact in the improvement of rapid fiber optic organizations in the country. IIJ gives a scope of administrations, including broadband web access, server farm administrations, and distributed computing.

Japan has been at the bleeding edge of fiber optic organization, and IIJ's endeavors have added to the inescapable accessibility of gigabit-speed web associations for both private and business clients.

South Korea's KT Enterprise:

KT Organization, previously known as Korea Telecom, is a main South Korean broadcast communications organization that has been instrumental in the far and wide reception of fiber optic organizations in the country. South Korea brags some the quickest web speeds internationally, because of broad fiber optic framework. KT Company's endeavors play had an essential impact in changing South Korea into a worldwide forerunner in broadband network, supporting administrations, for example, top quality streaming, web based gaming, and shrewd city drives.

Australia's Public Broadband Organization (NBN):

Australia's NBN is an administration driven drive pointed toward overhauling the nation's current media communications foundation. The task includes the organization of fiber optic organizations to give high velocity broadband admittance to homes and organizations across Australia. While the NBN has confronted difficulties and contentions connected with its rollout, it addresses a thorough work to improve web network and scaffold the computerized partition in a geologically different country.

China's Broadband China Drive:

China has attempted aggressive drives to grow and overhaul its broadband foundation to help the country's fast computerized change. The Broadband China Drive centers around sending fiber optic organizations to metropolitan and provincial regions the same, expecting to give high velocity web admittance to a huge number of families. The

WEB AT SPEED FIBER WONDERS

drive lines up with China's more extensive objectives of progressing computerized advancements, cultivating development, and supporting monetary development.

Norway's Altibox:

Altibox is a Norwegian broadcast communications organization that has earned respect for its fiber optic broadband administrations. Working in association with various regions, Altibox has effectively conveyed fiber-to-the-home (FTTH) organizations, offering fast web, advanced television, and voice administrations. Norway's obligation to fiber optic foundation has situated it as one of the nations with broad fiber inclusion, empowering occupants to appreciate solid and super quick network.

CityFibre (Joined Realm):

CityFibre is a UK-put together organization centered with respect to building and extending fiber optic organizations in different urban communities across the Unified Realm. The organization accomplices with nearby specialists and organizations to convey full-fiber foundation, expecting to address the interest for quicker and more solid availability.

CityFibre's drives add to the UK's endeavors to change from customary copper-based organizations to gigabit-speed fiber optic associations, supporting the country's computerized aspirations.

B4RN (Broadband for the Rustic North, Joined Realm):

B4RN is a local area driven drive in the Unified Realm that epitomizes the groundbreaking force of fiber optic organizations in country regions. Baffled by the absence of high velocity web choices, neighborhood networks met up to make B4RN, a local area interest organization that forms and works fiber optic organizations. B4RN shows how local area drove endeavors can defeat difficulties and bring rapid broadband to regions that may be underserved by conventional business suppliers.

New Zealand's Super Quick Broadband (UFB) Drive:

New Zealand's UFB drive is an administration driven program pointed toward conveying rapid fiber optic broadband to metropolitan and rustic regions. Sent off in organization with the confidential area, the drive includes the arrangement of fiber-to-the-home organizations, giving New Zealanders quicker web speeds. The UFB drive adds to the country's advanced change and supports different areas, including instruction, medical care, and business.

These true models feature the different applications and advantages of fruitful fiber optic organizations. Whether driven by government drives, confidential area ventures, or local area drove endeavors, these organizations have become necessary to current cultures, encouraging advancement, financial turn of events, and worked on personal satisfaction. The examples of overcoming adversity exhibit the extraordinary effect of fast, solid web availability in tending to the developing necessities of people, organizations, and whole countries. As the world keeps on progressing carefully, the job of fiber optic organizations in forming the fate of correspondence and availability stays vital.

Effective fiber optic organizations have turned into the foundation of present day correspondence framework, reforming the manner in which we associate, impart, and access data. These organizations, utilizing progressed fiber optic innovation, have exhibited their groundbreaking effect across different areas, giving fast, solid network to people, organizations, and whole networks. Looking at genuine instances of fruitful fiber optic organizations uncovers key bits of knowledge into their applications, benefits, and the critical job they play in molding the advanced scene.

One vital example of overcoming adversity is Google Fiber in the US. Sent off in 2012 in Kansas City and hence extending to a few urban communities the nation over, Google Fiber offers gigabit-speed internet providers. This drive has re-imagined web speed guidelines as well as driven rivalry in the broadband market.

By focusing on moderateness and client care, Google Fiber has impacted other specialist organizations to upgrade their organizations and deal higher-speed choices. The progress of Google Fiber highlights the effect of fiber optic organizations in animating advancement and increasing present expectations for web availability.

Singapore's Cross country Broadband Organization (NBN) is one more praiseworthy instance of an administration drove drive pointed toward giving high velocity broadband admittance to occupants and organizations. Conveyed in numerous stages, Singapore's NBN uses fiber optic innovation to convey super quick web availability. This drive has not just situated Singapore as one of the most associated countries internationally however has likewise upheld a great many administrations, including working from home, e-learning, and savvy city applications. The progress of Singapore's NBN features the significance of a far reaching way to deal with cross country fiber optic sending in encouraging computerized headways.

Web Drive Japan (IIJ) in Japan plays had a urgent impact in the far and wide reception of fiber optic organizations. As a main web access supplier, IIJ offers broadband web access, server farm administrations, and distributed computing. Japan has been at the front of fiber optic sending, and IIJ's endeavors have added to the country's standing for having probably the quickest web speeds worldwide. The outcome of IIJ features how a pledge to fast network can drive mechanical progressions and position a country as a forerunner in the worldwide computerized scene.

South Korea's KT Partnership has been instrumental in making South Korea a worldwide forerunner in broadband network. Utilizing fiber optic organizations, South Korea brags some the quickest web speeds around the world. KT Organization's endeavors play had a urgent impact in changing the country's computerized framework, supporting administrations, for example, superior quality streaming, web based gaming, and brilliant city drives. The progress of KT Company represents how key interests in fiber optic innovation can drive a country to the front of the computerized upset.

Australia's Public Broadband Organization (NBN) addresses an administration driven drive to update the country's broadcast communications foundation. In spite of confronting difficulties and discussions, the NBN highlights a far reaching work to upgrade web network across different geological districts. The sending of fiber optic organizations as a component of the NBN drive plans to connect the computerized partition and give rapid broadband admittance to homes and organizations. Australia's involvement in the NBN features the intricacies engaged with huge scope fiber optic sending projects and the significance of adjusting to developing mechanical and calculated difficulties.

China's Broadband China Drive embodies the country's aggressive endeavors to extend and update its broadband framework. Zeroed in on conveying fiber optic organizations to metropolitan and provincial regions the same, the drive expects to give rapid web admittance to a huge number of families.

Lined up with more extensive objectives of progressing computerized innovations and supporting monetary development, China's drive represents how a country's obligation to broad fiber optic organization can have sweeping ramifications for advancement and network.

Norway's Altibox has earned respect for giving rapid fiber optic broadband administrations. Working in association with various regions, Altibox conveys fiber-to-the-home organizations, offering high velocity web, computerized television, and voice administrations. Norway's obligation to broad fiber inclusion through drives like Altibox positions the country as a forerunner in solid and super quick network. Altibox's prosperity shows the way that coordinated effort between confidential substances and neighborhood networks can drive fiber optic sending and address the availability needs of different populaces.

CityFibre in the Assembled Realm is effectively fabricating and growing fiber optic organizations in different urban communities the nation over. The organization teams up with nearby specialists and organizations to convey full-fiber foundation, adding to the UK's progress from conventional copper-based organizations to gigabit-speed fiber optic associations. CityFibre's drives line up with the UK's computerized aspirations and show the significance of private-area contribution in propelling high velocity availability.

B4RN (Broadband for the Rustic North) in the Unified Realm addresses a local area driven drive that brings high velocity broadband to provincial regions. Baffled by the absence of fast web choices, neighborhood networks met up to make B4RN, a local area interest organization constructing and working fiber optic organizations. B4RN embodies how grassroots endeavors can defeat moves and carry fast network to regions that may be underserved by customary business suppliers. This people group driven model fills in as a motivation for tending to network differences in country areas.

Australia's Super Quick Broadband (UFB) drive is an administration driven program expecting to give rapid fiber optic broadband to metropolitan and country regions. Sent off in organization with the confidential area, the drive includes conveying fiber-to-the-home organizations, supporting New Zealand's computerized change. The UFB drive delineates how coordinated effort between general society and confidential areas can drive huge scope fiber optic organization, adding to financial turn of events and worked on advanced administrations.

These true models feature the different applications and advantages of fruitful fiber optic organizations. Whether driven by government drives, confidential area ventures, or local area drove endeavors, these organizations have become indispensable to present day cultures, cultivating advancement, financial turn of events, and worked on personal satisfaction. The examples of overcoming adversity show the extraordinary effect of fast, dependable web availability in tending to the advancing necessities of people, organizations, and whole countries. As the world keeps on progressing carefully, the job of fiber optic organizations in molding the fate of correspondence and availability stays essential.

Chapter 4

Connecting Communities: Fiber to the Home (FTTH)

The appearance of Fiber to the Home (FTTH) innovation has introduced another time of availability, generally changing the manner in which networks connect and convey. As the interest for rapid web keeps on flooding, FTTH has arisen as a progressive arrangement, giving unrivaled information transmission capacities. This groundbreaking innovation has the ability to connect the advanced gap, upgrade financial open doors, and cultivate local area development.

At its center, FTTH includes the organization of optical fiber links straightforwardly to individual homes and organizations, empowering gigabit-speed web access. Not at all like customary copper-based broadband innovations, FTTH disposes of the limits forced by transmission capacity limitations, offering a balanced and powerful association that can uphold both transfer and download speeds at remarkable levels. The consistent mix of fiber optics into the texture of networks is reshaping the scene of present day living.

One of the vital benefits of FTTH is its capacity to convey fast, low-inertness web associations, furnishing clients with a vivid internet based insight. From streaming superior quality substance to participating continuously video conferencing, the advantages of FTTH reach out past simple comfort. The dependability and speed of FTTH open ways to a horde of potential outcomes, from remote work and instruction to telehealth administrations, improving the regular routines of people and reinforcing the social texture of networks.

With regards to monetary turn of events, FTTH assumes a urgent part in encouraging development and business venture. Fast web access is at this point not an extravagance yet a need for organizations trying to flourish in the computerized age. The unwavering quality and speed of FTTH engage ventures to embrace cloud-based advancements, influence information examination, and take part in the worldwide computerized economy. This network goes about as an impetus for financial development, drawing in organizations, and driving position creation inside networks.

As people group become more interconnected through FTTH, the idea of brilliant urban communities picks up speed. The coordination of fiber optics takes into consideration the arrangement of savvy framework, including clever transportation frameworks, energy-effective structures, and high level public administrations. FTTH fills in as the spine for the Web of Things (IoT), empowering consistent correspondence among gadgets and working with the making of additional effective and economical metropolitan conditions.

The organization of FTTH isn't without its difficulties, be that as it may. The underlying expenses of laying fiber optic links can be significant, and the interaction might include disturbances to existing foundation. Neighborhood legislatures, specialist co-ops, and networks should team up to explore these provokes and guarantee a smooth change to FTTH. Public-private associations and local area commitment are fundamental to conquering obstructions and understanding the drawn out advantages of this groundbreaking innovation.

Notwithstanding monetary and innovative contemplations, the social effect of FTTH couldn't possibly be more significant. Admittance to high velocity web can possibly democratize data and training, restricting the advanced split that exists among metropolitan and country regions. FTTH engages people with the apparatuses to get to online instructive assets, partake in virtual study halls, and gain new abilities, regardless of their geographic area. This inclusivity cultivates a feeling of local area and equivalent chance for all.

The meaning of FTTH stretches out past public lines, with worldwide ramifications for network and correspondence. In an undeniably interconnected world, the capacity to trade data flawlessly is a foundation of global cooperation. FTTH reinforces the underpinnings of worldwide correspondence organizations, working with cross-line associations, and encouraging a more interconnected and cooperative worldwide local area.

In the domain of medical care, FTTH can possibly reform the conveyance of clinical benefits. Telehealth administrations, empowered by rapid web associations, permit patients to get to medical services experts from a distance, diminishing the requirement for actual travel and expanding the productivity of medical services conveyance. This is especially significant in rustic and underserved regions where admittance to clinical offices might be restricted. FTTH arises as a help, interfacing people to medical care assets and further developing generally wellbeing results.

The ecological effect of FTTH is likewise a critical thought. While the organization of fiber optic links requires an underlying venture of assets, the drawn out benefits incorporate energy productivity and decreased natural effect. Dissimilar to conventional copper-based networks, FTTH creates less sign misfortune and requires less energy for transmission. This proficiency adds to a more practical and eco-accommodating way to deal with network, lining up with worldwide endeavors to address environmental change and diminish carbon impressions.

Regardless of its various benefits, the reception of FTTH isn't uniform across all networks. Differences in foundation advancement, monetary assets, and administrative structures can make boundaries to passage for certain districts. Spanning this computerized partition requires deliberate endeavors from state run administrations, confidential area substances, and local area pioneers. Drives that focus on inclusivity, moderateness, and availability are critical to guaranteeing that the advantages of FTTH arrive at all portions of society.

The development of FTTH is entwined with headways in broadcast communications innovation. The change from conventional copper-based organizations to fiber optics addresses a jump forward in the mission for quicker, more solid, and versatile network. As innovative work proceed, the potential for considerably higher information transmission speeds and improved capacities turns into a reality. The ceaseless development in FTTH innovation guarantees that networks stay at the front of the advanced unrest.

In the domain of schooling, FTTH has the ability to reshape the manner in which understudies learn and instructors educate. The availability of fast web takes into consideration the consistent incorporation of advanced assets, online coordinated effort, and intelligent growth opportunities. Whether in customary homerooms or virtual conditions, FTTH makes a framework that upholds the advancing requirements of training in the 21st 100 years. The capacity to get to an abundance of data at high velocities upgrades the instructive experience, planning understudies for a universally associated and data driven future.

The social elements inside networks are additionally impacted by the coming of FTTH. The capacity to interface with others flawlessly, whether through virtual entertainment, video conferencing, or online discussions, rises above geological limits. FTTH works with the production of virtual networks, where people with shared interests or objectives can meet up, team up, and support one another. This feeling of interconnectedness cultivates social attachment and fortifies the social texture of networks.

With regards to catastrophe flexibility and reaction, FTTH ends up being a basic resource. The vigorous and solid nature of fiber optic associations guarantees that correspondence foundation stays in one piece even despite cataclysmic events or crises. In the midst of emergency, the capacity to impart really is principal for planning crisis reaction endeavors, spreading data to the general population, and offering help to those out of luck. FTTH turns into a life saver, empowering networks to remain associated and versatile in testing conditions.

The job of states in working with the arrangement of FTTH couldn't possibly be more significant. Policymakers assume a critical part in establishing an empowering climate that supports interest in fiber optic foundation. This includes creating guidelines that help the development of FTTH organizations, advancing solid rivalry among specialist co-ops, and boosting private area venture. Government drives that focus on advanced incorporation and foundation improvement add to the general progress of FTTH organization.

As FTTH turns out to be more pervasive, the customary models of metropolitan and country advancement are being reclassified. The geographic area of a local area no longer directs its degree of network or admittance to potential open doors. FTTH can possibly make everything fair, engaging country networks to take part in the advanced economy and access similar assets as their metropolitan partners. This change in elements has significant ramifications for the evenhanded dispersion of monetary open doors and the general improvement of social orders.

The security ramifications of FTTH can't be neglected. As people group become more dependent on high velocity web for basic administrations and correspondence, the requirement for hearty network protection measures becomes vital. Getting the respectability and protection of information sent over FTTH networks is fundamental to forestall digital dangers and defend the interests of people and organizations. Joint effort between state run administrations, network safety specialists, and specialist organizations is pivotal to creating and executing viable security conventions.

In the domain of diversion and media utilization, FTTH opens up additional opportunities for content conveyance. The fast, low-inactivity nature of fiber optic associations takes into account the consistent web based of superior quality video, augmented reality encounters, and vivid gaming. This change in the manner content is consumed has suggestions for the media business, driving development and testing conventional conveyance models. FTTH turns into an impetus for the development of diversion, offering shoppers remarkable decisions and encounters.

The effect of FTTH on land and property estimations is an essential part of its impact on networks. Admittance to rapid web has turned into a vital thought for homebuyers and organizations while picking an area. Networks with FTTH foundation are bound to draw in occupants and undertakings looking for solid and quick web availability. Accordingly, property estimations in regions with FTTH organization might encounter a vertical pattern, making monetary advantages for mortgage holders and adding to the general improvement of the local area.

With regards to security, the expanded network worked with by FTTH raises worries about the assortment and utilization of individual information. As additional gadgets become associated with the web, the potential for information breaks and security encroachments develops. Networks and policymakers really should lay out clear rules and guidelines that safeguard the protection privileges of people while advancing the advantages of FTTH. Adjusting the benefits of availability with the requirement for security shields is fundamental for the mindful arrangement of FTTH.

The future development of FTTH is probably going to be formed by arising innovations like 5G and the Web of Things (IoT). The coordination of these innovations with fiber optic organizations makes a synergistic environment that upgrades network, empowers new applications, and drives development. The blend of FTTH, 5G, and IoT makes ready for brilliant, associated networks that influence the force of information and innovation to upgrade the personal satisfaction for inhabitants.

As people group embrace the capability of FTTH, the significance of computerized proficiency turns out to be progressively apparent.

Guaranteeing that people have the right stuff and information to explore the advanced scene is pivotal for expanding the advantages of high velocity web access. Instructive drives, preparing projects, and local area outreach endeavors assume an imperative part in engaging occupants with the devices to outfit the maximum capacity of FTTH and take part definitively in the computerized age.

All in all, the organization of Fiber to the Home (FTTH) is a groundbreaking power that interfaces networks in manners beforehand unbelievable. The fast, low-inactivity nature of fiber optic associations changes the elements of correspondence, training, medical services, and monetary turn of events. As people group become more interconnected, the social texture is reinforced, and new open doors for coordinated effort and development arise.

While the reception of FTTH presents difficulties, the drawn out benefits are certain. State run administrations, confidential area substances, and networks should cooperate to beat boundaries to section, guaranteeing that the upsides of FTTH arrive at all portions of society. The constant development of FTTH innovation, combined with headways in media communications, guarantees a future where network is consistent, solid, and comprehensive.

The ramifications of FTTH reach out past the domains of innovation and framework. They address the actual quintessence of local area advancement, impacting how people live, work, and communicate with each other. FTTH can possibly span the computerized partition, enable networks, and make ready for an additional interconnected and prosperous future. As the world hugs the time of Fiber to the Home, the excursion towards genuinely associated networks unfurls, offering a brief look into a future where the potential outcomes are boundless.

4.1 The concept of bringing fiber directly to individual homes

The idea of bringing fiber straightforwardly to individual homes, usually known as Fiber to the Home (FTTH), addresses a progressive change in outlook in the domain of broadcast communications and network. At its center, FTTH includes the organization of fiber optic links that straightforwardly interface individual homes and organizations to a rapid web organization. This takeoff from customary broadband advances, for example, Computerized Endorser Line (DSL) or satellite web, achieves a large group of extraordinary advantages that stretch out past simple upgrades in web speed.

The central guideline of FTTH spins around the utilization of fiber optic links, which are made out of flimsy strands of glass or plastic that communicate information utilizing beats of light. This innovation empowers the conveyance of essentially higher transmission capacities contrasted with customary copper-based links, bringing about quicker and more solid web associations. The choice to bring fiber straightforwardly to homes mirrors a pledge to furnishing clients with an even and vigorous web insight, described by high transfer and download speeds.

One of the essential benefits of FTTH is its capacity to convey gigabit-speed web access. Dissimilar to conventional broadband innovations that might have limits on how much information that can be sent over a given period, FTTH gives clients unrivaled speed and

responsiveness. This rapid network opens up a horde of potential outcomes, from consistent spilling of superior quality substance to constant internet based joint effort, establishing a climate where clients can completely use the capacities of the computerized age.

The organization of FTTH is definitely not a one-size-fits-all arrangement yet rather a versatile and versatile methodology that can be custom-made to the requirements of different networks. The execution of FTTH organizations might shift in scale, going from little rustic networks to thickly populated metropolitan regions. The choice to put resources into FTTH framework is frequently impacted by variables like populace thickness, existing media communications foundation, and the financial practicality of sending.

The monetary advantages of FTTH are significant and complex. According to a macroeconomic viewpoint, the sending of fiber optic organizations can invigorate monetary development by encouraging development, drawing in organizations, and making position. Rapid web access is progressively perceived as a basic calculate deciding the seriousness of districts in the worldwide economy. Organizations that work in regions with strong FTTH framework gain an upper hand by approaching quicker and more solid network, empowering them to use cloud-based innovations, manage consistent web-based exchanges, and take part in the computerized commercial center.

Notwithstanding its monetary effect, FTTH can possibly reclassify the scene of training. The idea of "schoolwork" is changed as understudies get close enough to fast web at home, empowering them to participate in web-based research, team up on projects, and partake in virtual study halls. This shift towards a more associated and carefully improved instructive experience plans understudies for the requests of an information driven economy. In any case, it is pivotal to resolve issues of advanced value and guarantee that all understudies, no matter what their geographic area or financial status, approach the advantages of FTTH.

Medical services is one more area where the effect of FTTH is progressively critical. The appearance of telehealth administrations, worked with by high velocity web network, permits people to get to clinical meetings, get remote observing, and participate in virtual medical care administrations. This is especially significant in provincial or underserved regions where admittance to medical services offices might be restricted. FTTH turns into a urgent empowering influence of medical care conveyance, adding to worked on persistent results and a more effective medical services framework.

The social ramifications of FTTH reach out to the idea of local area improvement. As people and families get sufficiently close to rapid web, the manner in which they interface with each other and take part in the computerized world goes through a change. Virtual people group, conformed to shared interests or objectives, become more common.

Whether through web-based entertainment, online gatherings, or cooperative stages, FTTH works with the formation of interconnected computerized networks, encouraging a feeling of having a place and shared encounters.

The organization of FTTH additionally adds to the improvement of brilliant urban areas. As fiber optic organizations are coordinated into the metropolitan framework, urban communities can execute wise frameworks that improve effectiveness, manageability, and the general personal satisfaction for occupants. Brilliant transportation frameworks, energy-proficient structures, and high level public administrations become practical through the rapid and low-idleness abilities of FTTH. The Web of Things (IoT) environment, where gadgets impart flawlessly, is dependent on the vigorous availability given by FTTH.

Be that as it may, the reception of FTTH isn't without its difficulties. One of the essential obstacles is the underlying expense related with laying fiber optic links. The sending of FTTH framework requires huge interest in materials, work, and innovation. Neighborhood state run administrations, media communications organizations, and different partners should team up to explore these monetary difficulties and foster practical models for financing and carrying out FTTH projects. Public-private organizations and local area commitment become urgent parts of effective FTTH sending.

Besides, the actual organization of FTTH foundation can introduce calculated and administrative difficulties. Removal and establishment exercises might disturb existing foundation, presenting transitory burdens to networks. Successful coordination between broadcast communications suppliers and neighborhood specialists is fundamental to limit disturbances and guarantee a smooth progress to FTTH. Guidelines that smooth out the allowing system and work with the organization of fiber optic organizations assume a urgent part in defeating these difficulties.

With regards to computerized consideration, tending to the computerized partition is a basic part of FTTH sending. The advantages of fast web access ought to be open to all citizenry, regardless of their geographic area or financial status. Drives that attention on reasonableness, availability, and computerized education are fundamental to guarantee that the upsides of FTTH reach underserved and minimized networks. Spanning the computerized partition adds to a more impartial circulation of chances and assets.

Ecological contemplations additionally become possibly the most important factor while assessing the maintainability of FTTH. While the underlying creation and establishment of fiber optic links might have an ecological effect, the drawn out benefits incorporate energy productivity and diminished carbon impression. Contrasted with conventional copper-based networks, FTTH requires less energy for transmission and delivers less sign misfortune. This effectiveness lines up with worldwide endeavors to address environmental change and advance naturally economical innovations.

According to a security point of view, the rising dependence on fast web for basic administrations raises worries about network safety. As people group become more associated through FTTH, the requirement for strong network protection measures becomes principal. Safeguarding the honesty and protection of information sent over fiber optic organizations is fundamental to forestall digital dangers and guarantee the security of people and organizations. Coordinated effort between state run administrations, network protection specialists, and specialist organizations is significant for creating and carrying out compelling security conventions.

Looking towards the future, the development of FTTH is intently attached to progressions in broadcast communications innovation. The coordination of 5G innovation and the extension of the IoT environment further upgrade the capacities of FTTH organizations. The mix of FTTH, 5G, and IoT establishes a synergistic climate where network turns out to be significantly more consistent, empowering new applications and driving development. As innovation keeps on propelling, the potential for higher information transmission speeds and improved capacities in FTTH networks turns into a reality.

In the domain of diversion and media utilization, FTTH significantly affects content conveyance. The rapid and low-inertness nature of fiber optic associations empower the consistent web based of superior quality video, augmented reality encounters, and vivid gaming. This change in the manner content is consumed has suggestions for the media business, driving advancement in happy creation, conveyance, and utilization. FTTH turns into an impetus for the development of diversion, offering purchasers exceptional decisions and encounters.

Land and property estimations are additionally impacted by the arrangement of FTTH framework. Admittance to high velocity web is progressively turning into a vital thought for homebuyers and organizations while picking an area. Networks with hearty FTTH networks are bound to draw in occupants and ventures looking for dependable and quick web availability. Thus, property estimations in regions with FTTH arrangement might encounter a vertical pattern, making financial advantages for mortgage holders and adding to the general improvement of the local area.

4.2 Benefits of FTTH for end-users

Fiber to the Home (FTTH) innovation has arisen as a groundbreaking power in the domain of broadcast communications, offering end-clients a large group of advantages that reclassify the manner in which people insight and cooperate with the computerized world. The sending of fiber optic links straightforwardly to individual homes has made ready for phenomenal web rates, unwavering quality, and a large number of utilizations that upgrade different parts of day to day existence.

One of the essential advantages of FTTH for end-clients is the noteworthy improvement in web speed. Conventional broadband advances, for example, Computerized Endorser Line (DSL) and digital web, frequently experience constraints as far as how much information that can be sent over a given period. Conversely, FTTH gives even high velocity web access, implying that both transfer and download speeds are essentially quicker and more steady. This means faster stacking times for pages, consistent gushing of top quality substance, and a generally speaking upgraded internet based insight for end-clients.

The balanced idea of FTTH is especially favorable for exercises that require hearty transfer speeds, for example, video conferencing, online coordinated effort, and record sharing. In a period where remote work and virtual gatherings have become progressively predominant, FTTH engages end-clients to take part in video meetings without buffering issues or slack, encouraging a more consistent and useful virtual cooperation experience. This is a pivotal part of the developing work scene, where people and organizations the same rely upon dependable and high velocity web associations.

Notwithstanding further developed speed, the dependability of FTTH is a champion component for end-clients. Fiber optic links are less defenseless to outer obstruction and ecological variables, making them stronger and solid than conventional copper-based links. This expanded dependability guarantees that end-clients experience negligible disturbances in their web access, prompting a more steady and reliable web-based insight. Whether for work, training, or diversion, the dependability of FTTH adds to a feeling of certainty and confidence in the network framework.

The groundbreaking effect of FTTH stretches out to the domain of amusement and media utilization. With rapid and low-dormancy network, end-clients can flawlessly transfer superior quality video content, take part in web based gaming without idleness issues, and investigate vivid augmented simulation encounters. The disposal of buffering and defers improves the general diversion experience, permitting clients to appreciate content continuously without the disappointment of interferences. As the interest for data transmission serious applications develops, FTTH positions end-clients to embrace the potential outcomes of advanced amusement completely.

The ramifications of FTTH for online instruction are especially imperative. As instructive foundations progressively embrace computerized stages for learning, the requirement for rapid and dependable web access becomes central. FTTH enables understudies to take part in virtual homerooms, access online instructive assets, and participate in cooperative ventures with peers, regardless of their geographic area. This inclusivity is critical for democratizing training and guaranteeing that all understudies have equivalent admittance to the amazing open doors presented by advanced learning conditions.

Medical care administrations have likewise encountered a change in outlook with the coming of FTTH. Telehealth administrations, empowered by rapid web availability, permit end-clients to get to clinical meetings, get remote observing, and take part in virtual medical care administrations from the solace of their homes. This is especially useful for people in country or underserved regions where admittance to medical care offices might be restricted. FTTH arises as a life saver, interfacing patients to medical care experts and administrations, in this manner further developing medical care openness and results.

The monetary ramifications of FTTH for end-clients are huge. Rapid web access is presently not an extravagance however a need for people trying to flourish in the computerized economy. Whether for remote work, online business venture, or support in the gig economy, FTTH enables end-clients with the apparatuses to use advanced stages and administrations. The unwavering quality and speed of FTTH add to the productivity of online exchanges, the utilization of cloud-based advances, and by and large monetary cooperation in the computerized commercial center.

The idea of shrewd homes is another region where FTTH finishes unmistakable advantages up clients. With the strong availability given by fiber optic links, end-clients can consistently incorporate brilliant gadgets and home mechanization frameworks into their residing spaces. From savvy indoor regulators and lighting frameworks to surveillance cameras and voice-actuated partners, FTTH establishes a climate where gadgets convey flawlessly, upgrading comfort, energy productivity, and in general personal satisfaction for end-clients.

The social ramifications of FTTH are reflected in the manner people associate with each other and take part in computerized networks. The rapid and low-idleness nature of FTTH works with continuous correspondence through video calls, virtual entertainment, and online discussions. Virtual people group, conformed to shared interests or objectives, become more common as FTTH empowers people to take part in cooperative tasks, gaming networks, and social collaborations without the constraints of slow web speeds. The feeling of interconnectedness cultivates social union and fortifies the social texture of networks.

Computerized consideration, a vital part of the advantages of FTTH, addresses the basic to connect the computerized partition. FTTH guarantees that high velocity web access is open to all citizenry, no matter what their geographic area or financial status. Drives that emphasis on moderateness, openness, and computerized proficiency assume a fundamental part in guaranteeing that the upsides of FTTH reach underserved and underestimated networks. By tending to the computerized partition, FTTH adds to a more evenhanded dispersion of chances and assets.

From an ecological stance, the maintainability of FTTH is eminent. While the underlying creation and establishment of fiber optic links might have an ecological effect, the drawn out benefits incorporate energy proficiency and decreased carbon impression.

Contrasted with conventional copper-based networks, FTTH requires less energy for transmission and delivers less sign misfortune. This productivity lines up with worldwide endeavors to address environmental change and advance naturally manageable innovations, offering end-clients a network arrangement that is both mechanically progressed and earth capable.

In the domain of safety, FTTH guarantees that end-clients can partake in a solid web-based insight. The hearty and dependable nature of fiber optic associations improves the security of information communicated over FTTH organizations. As network safety concerns become progressively common in the computerized age, FTTH gives an establishment to get online exchanges, security of individual data, and by and large genuine serenity for end-clients. Coordinated effort between state run administrations, network safety specialists, and specialist organizations is critical for creating and executing compelling security conventions that shield the interests of people and organizations.

Looking towards the future, the development of FTTH is entwined with headways in broadcast communications innovation. The joining of 5G innovation and the development of the Web of Things (IoT) environment further upgrade the abilities of FTTH organizations. The mix of FTTH, 5G, and IoT establishes a synergistic climate where network turns out to be considerably more consistent, empowering new applications and driving development. As innovation keeps on propelling, end-clients can expect considerably higher information transmission speeds and upgraded capacities in FTTH organizations, situating them at the very front of the advanced unrest.

4.3 Communities with successful FTTH implementations

Networks that have effectively carried out Fiber to the Home (FTTH) foundation have encountered groundbreaking changes that stretch out across different features of life. From upgraded financial open doors and occupation creation to further developed instruction, medical care, and generally speaking personal satisfaction, the effect of fruitful FTTH executions reverberates profoundly inside these networks. Looking at the qualities and results of such executions gives significant bits of knowledge into the expected advantages and difficulties related with sending FTTH on a local area wide scale.

One of the critical signs of networks with effective FTTH executions is the significant effect on monetary turn of events. The organization of fiber optic organizations straightforwardly to homes and organizations makes an establishment for an energetic and serious nearby economy. Organizations working inside these networks get close enough to high velocity, solid web associations, empowering them to use cloud-based advances, go through with consistent internet based exchanges, and take part more actually in the computerized commercial center.

The expanded transmission capacity and availability presented by FTTH cultivate advancement and business venture. New companies and private ventures, specifically, benefit from the strong foundation, permitting them to contend on a level battleground with bigger partners. This powerful climate draws in organizations that focus on advanced network, prompting position creation and financial development inside the local area. The outcome of organizations dependent on fast internet providers becomes interlaced with the general success of the local area.

Notwithstanding financial contemplations, fruitful FTTH executions significantly affect instruction. Schools and instructive organizations inside these networks benefit from high velocity web access, permitting them to incorporate advanced innovations into the learning climate. Understudies get close enough to online instructive assets, take part in virtual study halls, and take part in cooperative ventures that set them up for a carefully determined future. FTTH establishes a climate where instructive open doors are not restricted by geological requirements, guaranteeing that understudies have equivalent admittance to an abundance of data and learning assets.

The idea of remote learning is essentially upgraded in networks with fruitful FTTH executions. As the interest for adaptable and remote work choices develops, the capacity for understudies to take part in virtual study halls turns out to be progressively urgent. FTTH guarantees that understudies in these networks can flawlessly partake in web based opportunities for growth, team up with friends, and access instructive substance without the constraints of more slow web speeds. This inclusivity adds to a more evenhanded dispersion of instructive open doors.

The effect of fruitful FTTH executions on medical care administrations is similarly significant. Telehealth administrations, empowered by rapid web network, permit occupants in these networks to get to clinical counsels, get remote checking, and take part in virtual medical care administrations. This is especially gainful in rustic or underserved regions where admittance to medical care offices might be restricted. FTTH turns into a basic empowering influence of medical services conveyance, adding to worked on persistent results and a more effective medical services framework.

The social texture of networks with effective FTTH executions is fortified by the expanded availability and correspondence capacities. Virtual people group, conformed to shared interests or objectives, become more common as FTTH empowers occupants to participate in cooperative ventures, social connections, and online gatherings without the limits of slow web speeds. The feeling of interconnectedness encourages social union and makes an energetic computerized local area where people can interface and backing one another, independent of actual closeness.

Brilliant city drives frequently track down fruitful ground in networks with effective FTTH executions. The joining of fiber optic organizations takes into account the sending of insightful framework, including shrewd transportation frameworks, energy-productive structures, and high level public administrations. FTTH fills in as the spine for the Web of Things (IoT), empowering consistent correspondence among gadgets and working with the making of additional productive and supportable metropolitan conditions. The network given by FTTH turns into an impetus for the improvement of savvy urban communities that focus on effectiveness, supportability, and personal satisfaction for occupants.

The land scene is additionally affected by fruitful FTTH executions. Admittance to high velocity web turns into a critical variable for homebuyers and organizations while picking an area. Networks with powerful FTTH networks are bound to draw in occupants and endeavors looking for solid and quick web availability. Accordingly, property estimations in regions with effective FTTH executions might encounter a vertical pattern, making monetary advantages for mortgage holders and adding to the general improvement of the local area.

The financial and social advantages of FTTH stretch out past public lines, with worldwide ramifications for availability and correspondence. In an undeniably interconnected world, the capacity to trade data flawlessly is a foundation of global cooperation. Networks with effective FTTH executions become center points of development and joint effort, drawing in organizations, analysts, and business people from around the world. This worldwide interconnectedness positions these networks at the bleeding edge of the computerized insurgency, adding to the headway of innovation and information on a worldwide scale.

In spite of the various benefits, the execution of FTTH isn't without its difficulties. Fruitful FTTH organizations require vital preparation, coordinated effort among partners, and a pledge to beating expected deterrents. The underlying interest in laying fiber optic links can be significant, and the cycle might include disturbances to existing foundation. Nearby states, specialist organizations, and networks should cooperate to explore these provokes and guarantee a smooth change to FTTH.

Public-private organizations assume a vital part in the outcome of FTTH executions. States and confidential area elements should team up to create and execute arrangements that help the extension of FTTH organizations. Guidelines that smooth out the allowing system and boost private area speculation add to the general progress of FTTH organizations. Local area commitment is similarly fundamental, as occupants assume a vital part in the acknowledgment and reception of FTTH foundation.

The progress of FTTH executions is in many cases dependent upon resolving issues of advanced value and consideration. While FTTH brings various advantages, it is basic to guarantee that all inhabitants, no matter what their financial status, approach high velocity internet providers.

Drives that attention on moderateness, availability, and computerized education are vital for span the advanced separation and guarantee that the benefits of FTTH arrive at all fragments of society. Inclusivity turns into a core value in fruitful FTTH executions, guaranteeing that the advantages of network are shared by the whole local area.

Ecological contemplations likewise become possibly the most important factor while assessing the manageability of FTTH executions. While the underlying creation and establishment of fiber optic links might have a natural effect, the drawn out benefits incorporate energy proficiency and diminished ecological effect. FTTH requires less energy for transmission and creates less sign misfortune contrasted with customary copper-based networks. This proficiency lines up with worldwide endeavors to address environmental change and diminish carbon impressions, settling on FTTH a feasible decision for networks looking towards an all the more earth dependable future.

Security contemplations are vital in effective FTTH executions. As people group become more dependent on rapid web for basic administrations and correspondence, the requirement for powerful network protection measures becomes fundamental. Safeguarding the uprightness and protection of information communicated over FTTH networks is fundamental to forestall digital dangers and shield the interests of people and organizations. Cooperation between state run administrations, network protection specialists, and specialist organizations is urgent for creating and executing compelling security conventions that guarantee the solid and dependable utilization of FTTH framework.

Looking towards the future, the advancement of FTTH is probably going to be molded by arising innovations like 5G and the Web of Things (IoT). The reconciliation of these advancements with fiber optic organizations makes a synergistic biological system that upgrades network, empowers new applications, and drives development. As innovative work proceed, the potential for considerably higher information transmission speeds and upgraded capacities turns into a reality. The consistent development in FTTH innovation guarantees that networks with fruitful executions stay at the very front of the computerized transformation.

4.4 Addressing challenges in implementing FTTH projects

The execution of Fiber to the Home (FTTH) projects, while promising extraordinary advantages, accompanies its own arrangement of difficulties that partners should explore to guarantee effective organization. Tending to these difficulties requires a thorough comprehension of the intricacies engaged with laying fiber optic foundation, organizing with different partners, and beating monetary and administrative obstacles. In this investigation, we dig into the diverse difficulties related with carrying out FTTH projects and consider techniques to moderate these snags.

1. **Monetary Hindrances:**
   One of the essential difficulties in carrying out FTTH projects is the significant monetary speculation required. Laying fiber optic links to individual homes includes huge expenses for materials, work, and innovation. Neighborhood states, specialist co-ops, and financial backers should wrestle with the underlying capital expense, which can be a hindrance, particularly for more modest networks or locales with restricted monetary assets. To defeat this test, creative supporting models, like public-private organizations, can be investigated. Coordinated efforts between government organizations and confidential substances consider the sharing of expenses and dangers, making FTTH projects all the more monetarily feasible.

2. **Disturbance to Foundation:**
   The actual arrangement of FTTH foundation can prompt disturbances in existing framework, including streets, utilities, and public spaces. Unearthing and establishment exercises might burden occupants and disturb day to day existence in impacted regions. Powerful coordination between broadcast communications suppliers and neighborhood specialists is critical to limit interruptions and guarantee a smooth progress to FTTH. Clear correspondence with the local area in regards to the course of events, extension, and likely burdens of the task oversees

assumptions and cultivates a cooperative way to deal with address disturbance challenges.

3. **Administrative Obstacles:**
Exploring administrative structures is one more critical test in carrying out FTTH projects. Neighborhood guidelines, drafting regulations, and allowing processes differ, adding intricacy to the arrangement cycle. Smoothing out guidelines to work with the organization of fiber optic organizations is fundamental. States can assume a significant part in establishing an empowering climate by creating strategies that help FTTH execution, diminishing regulatory obstacles, and boosting private area speculation. Participating in proactive exchange with administrative specialists guarantees a reasonable comprehension of consistence necessities and works with a smoother execution process.

4. **Local area Opposition:**
Local area obstruction and resistance to FTTH ventures can emerge because of worries about interruptions, saw wellbeing dangers, or stylish contemplations. Conquering this challenge requires proactive local area commitment and instruction. Giving straightforward data about the advantages of FTTH, tending to worries through local area discussions, and including occupants in the dynamic cycle can assist with building trust and relieve opposition. Public mindfulness crusades featuring the drawn out benefits of fast web network add to cultivating local area support for FTTH projects.

5. **Advanced Incorporation and Reasonableness:**
Guaranteeing computerized consideration and moderateness is a basic test related with FTTH execution. The advantages of high velocity web ought to be available to all citizenry, regardless of their financial status.

Reasonableness concerns might restrict admittance to FTTH administrations for specific socioeconomics. To address this, state run administrations, specialist co-ops, and local area associations can team up to foster drives that emphasis on reasonableness, availability, and advanced proficiency. Sponsored or limited plans for low-pay families and designated instructive projects add to crossing over the computerized partition and guaranteeing inclusivity.

6. **Innovation and Framework Similarity:**
FTTH projects require similarity with existing innovation and framework. Now and again, networks might have inheritance frameworks or obsolete foundation that requirements moving up to oblige fiber optic organizations. Evaluating the similarity of existing foundation and anticipating important updates are fundamental stages in FTTH execution. Cooperation between media communications suppliers and neighborhood utilities guarantees a comprehensive way to deal with framework improvement, tending to similarity challenges and streamlining the joining of FTTH with existing frameworks.

7. **Long Endorsement Cycles:**
Extended endorsement processes, including natural effect appraisals and license endorsements, can altogether defer FTTH projects. Effective and smoothed out endorsement systems are fundamental to speed up execution without settling for less on natural and wellbeing norms. States can lay out committed teams or facilitated endorsement channels for FTTH projects, decreasing regulatory deferrals and speeding up the sending course of events. Focusing on framework projects that add to local area advancement supports opportune direction and execution.

8. **Ability Deficiencies and Labor force Preparing:**
The sending of FTTH framework requires gifted experts, including specialists, architects, and undertaking administrators. Ability deficiencies here can hinder the advancement of FTTH projects. Putting resources into labor force preparing programs, working together with instructive foundations, and setting out apprenticeship open doors address expertise deficiencies. This

not just guarantees a proficient labor force for progressing and future FTTH projects yet in addition adds to nearby monetary improvement by encouraging a talented work pool.

9. **Network protection Concerns:**
   As people group become more associated through FTTH, network protection turns into a principal concern. Safeguarding the honesty and protection of information sent over FTTH networks is fundamental to forestall digital dangers. Legislatures, specialist co-ops, and network protection specialists should team up to create and execute strong security conventions. Normal reviews, updates to security foundation, and public mindfulness crusades add to building a solid computerized climate for FTTH clients.

10. **Merchant and Innovation Determination:**
    Choosing reasonable sellers and innovations for FTTH projects is a basic choice that can influence the outcome of execution. Networks should cautiously assess likely merchants, taking into account factors like dependability, adaptability, and long haul support. Taking part in pilot projects, looking for proposals from different networks with fruitful executions, and leading careful assessments add to informed seller and innovation determinations. Adaptability in innovation decisions guarantees that FTTH framework stays versatile to future headways.

11. **Natural Effect:**
    The sending of FTTH framework, while offering long haul natural advantages, may have starting ecological effects. The creation and establishment of fiber optic links include asset utilization and energy use. To address this, networks can carry out naturally cognizant practices, like reusing and manageable obtaining of materials. Offsetting the ecological contact with the drawn out supportability benefits of FTTH requires an all encompassing methodology that thinks about both prompt worries and future advantages.

12. **Public Insight and Schooling:**
    Public discernment and comprehension of FTTH projects assume an essential part in their prosperity. Falsehood or absence of mindfulness can prompt distrust and opposition. Executing exhaustive state funded training efforts is fundamental to impart the advantages, disperse legends, and encourage local area support. Using different correspondence channels, including online entertainment, local area studios, and instructive materials, adds to making an educated and steady open discernment regarding FTTH projects.
13. **Versatility and Future-Sealing:**
    FTTH projects should be versatile and future-confirmation to oblige developing advances and expanding transmission capacity requests. Making arrangements for versatility guarantees that the framework can adjust to the developing necessities of the local area after some time. Cooperation with broadcast communications suppliers and standard evaluations of mechanical progressions add to future-sealing FTTH projects. Adaptability in plan and a forward-looking methodology empower networks to remain in front of mechanical turns of events and guarantee the life span of their FTTH framework.
14. **Local area Availability:**

Surveying the status of a local area for FTTH execution is a significant part of undertaking a good outcome. Factors like local area commitment, mindfulness, and eagerness to embrace new advancements add to status. Directing exhaustive preparation appraisals distinguishes likely provokes and takes into account designated intercessions to address explicit local area needs. Fitting correspondence procedures and training projects to the extraordinary qualities of every local area guarantees a more consistent and effective FTTH execution.

Chapter 5

Gigabit Cities and Beyond

As of late, the idea of Gigabit Urban communities has arisen as a groundbreaking power in the domain of metropolitan network and computerized foundation. Gigabit Urban communities, described by boundless admittance to gigabit-speed web, address a huge jump forward concerning broadband capacities. The expression "gigabit" alludes to information move paces of 1 gigabit each second (Gbps) or higher, a glaring difference to the more slow rates that numerous urban communities have customarily experienced. This flood in network opens up a universe of opportunities for occupants, organizations, and legislatures the same.

The underpinning of Gigabit Urban areas lies in the sending of high velocity fiber-optic organizations, which have the ability to communicate information at unquestionably quick rates. Fiber-optic innovation includes the utilization of flimsy glass or plastic strings to communicate information as beats of light, guaranteeing quick and effective information move. While customary broadband advancements, for example, Computerized Supporter Line (DSL) or link, have served metropolitan regions for quite a long time, they fail to measure up to the capacities of fiber-optic organizations.

The benefits of Gigabit Urban communities are multi-layered. One of the most prompt advantages is the improved web insight for inhabitants. With gigabit-speed web, exercises like web based superior quality recordings, internet gaming, and video conferencing become consistent and cushion free. This better nature of administration not just fulfills the requests of current advanced ways of life yet additionally opens up additional opportunities for schooling, amusement, and remote work.

Besides, Gigabit Urban communities assume a critical part in cultivating monetary development and advancement. Rapid web is an impetus for business venture and private company improvement, as it empowers quicker information moves, productive correspondence, and admittance to cloud-based administrations. In a time where computerized network is inseparable from financial seriousness, urban communities with gigabit framework are better situated to draw in organizations, speculation, and a talented labor force.

The meaning of Gigabit Urban communities stretches out past individual families and organizations. Civil legislatures can use fast availability to upgrade public administrations, carry out shrewd city drives, and work on by and large metropolitan effectiveness. From savvy traffic the executives frameworks to keen garbage removal arrangements, the reconciliation of gigabit-speed web permits urban communities to convey state of the art innovations that improve the personal satisfaction for occupants.

The excursion toward Gigabit Urban communities is a multi-layered try that includes joint effort among public and confidential elements. Network access suppliers (ISPs) assume a focal part in conveying the vital framework, however civil legislatures likewise contribute by establishing a helpful administrative climate and putting resources into the improvement of computerized foundation. The public-private organization model has demonstrated compelling in speeding up the rollout of gigabit organizations, with the two areas cooperating to connect the advanced gap.

As the idea of Gigabit Urban areas picks up speed, it is significant to consider the developing scene of computerized network. Past gigabit speeds, there is a developing accentuation on the improvement of organizations that can uphold significantly higher information move rates. The expression "past gigabit" embodies the following wilderness of availability, where paces of 10 gigabits each second (10 Gbps) or more become the new norm.

Past gigabit network addresses a change in perspective in the computerized scene, with the possibility to reform how we collaborate with innovation. The approach of advancements, for example, 5G and the constant development of fiber-optic organizations add to the acknowledgment of these remarkable velocities. The ramifications of such rapid network are immense and stretch out across different spaces, including medical services, instruction, amusement, and then some.

In the medical care area, the effect of past gigabit network is groundbreaking. Telemedicine, which has acquired noticeable quality as of late, stands to benefit fundamentally from quicker and more solid web speeds. Top quality video meetings, ongoing remote observing of patients, and the quick trade of clinical information become potential outcomes as well as real factors. Past gigabit network works with the consistent joining of innovation into medical services conveyance, upgrading patient consideration and further developing by and large well-being results.

Training is another field where past gigabit availability can rethink the opportunity for growth. The shift toward online instruction and e-learning stages has sped up, and fast web is an essential for a smooth and intuitive learning climate. Past gigabit speeds empower the conveyance of vivid instructive substance, support computer generated reality (VR) applications for upgraded opportunities for growth, and work with cooperation among understudies and instructors across the globe.

Media outlets is no more interesting to the effect of propelling availability. Past gigabit speeds introduce another period of superior grade, vivid substance conveyance. Web-based features can offer 4K as well as even 8K goal recordings without buffering, and computer generated reality encounters become more consistent and similar. The capacity to download enormous documents, for example, computer games or high-goal films, in no time further upgrades the purchaser experience.

As urban areas embrace the conceivable outcomes of past gigabit network, they position themselves at the cutting edge of mechanical development. The idea of brilliant urban communities, which influence information and availability to advance metropolitan tasks, turns out to be more achievable with the sped up and unwavering quality gave by past gigabit organizations. From clever transportation frameworks to constant natural checking, urban communities can execute a wide cluster of brilliant drives that upgrade supportability, productivity, and by and large reasonableness.

The way to past gigabit availability includes tending to different difficulties and contemplations. Framework sending is a complex and asset concentrated process that requires fastidious preparation and co-ordination. Beating actual boundaries, like troublesome landscape or existing foundation restrictions, requests inventive arrangements and a guarantee to long haul arranging. Moreover, issues of moderateness and advanced education should be addressed to guarantee that the advantages of past gigabit network are available to all sections of the populace.

Moreover, the security and protection ramifications of past gigabit availability can't be neglected. As information move speeds increment, the volume of information being sent additionally develops dramatically. This inundation of information requires strong network safety measures to safeguard against possible dangers and breaks. Urban communities should put resources into secure and versatile organizations, execute encryption conventions, and instruct inhabitants and organizations about prescribed procedures for online security.

In the domain of policymaking, legislatures assume a pivotal part in molding the direction of past gigabit network. Clear and ground breaking guidelines are fundamental to support private area interest in rapid foundation. Legislatures can likewise boost the improvement of creative advancements and plans of action that help the development toward past gigabit speeds. Joint effort between states, confidential area partners, and the scholastic local area is crucial for making a comprehensive and feasible system for the computerized future.

The worldwide scene of past gigabit availability is assorted, with various districts advancing at different speeds. While certain urban communities are at the very front of conveying gigabit and past gigabit foundation, others face moves in getting up to speed because of financial requirements or geological restrictions. Spanning the computerized partition requires purposeful endeavors from legislatures, industry players, and global associations to guarantee that each local area, no matter what its area or financial status, approaches fast web.

All in all, the development from Gigabit Urban areas to past gigabit network addresses a dynamic and extraordinary excursion in the domain of metropolitan availability. The organization of rapid web framework not just improves the computerized encounters of people and organizations yet additionally fills in as an impetus for monetary development, development, and the improvement of shrewd urban communities.

Past gigabit availability opens up new outskirts in medical care, training, amusement, and different areas, introducing a period of uncommon potential outcomes.

Be that as it may, the acknowledgment of past gigabit network accompanies its portion of difficulties, from the intricacies of foundation organization to the basic of resolving issues connected with security, protection, and advanced consideration. Legislatures, industry partners, and networks should work cooperatively to explore these difficulties and guarantee that the advantages of high velocity availability are fairly circulated.

As we look toward the future, the vision of past gigabit network offers a brief look into a carefully interconnected reality where the potential for development has no limits. The excursion toward this future is an aggregate undertaking that requires vital preparation, speculation, and a promise to building strong and comprehensive computerized environments. In embracing the open doors introduced by past gigabit availability, urban areas can situate themselves as centers of development, supportability, and thriving in the advanced age.

5.1 Exploring the concept of Gigabit cities

The idea of Gigabit Urban communities has arisen as an extraordinary power in the domain of metropolitan network and computerized foundation. Gigabit Urban communities, portrayed by boundless admittance to gigabit-speed web, address a huge jump forward concerning broadband capacities. The expression "gigabit" indicates information move paces of 1 gigabit each second (Gbps) or higher, a conspicuous difference to the more slow rates that numerous urban communities have generally experienced. This flood in network opens up a universe of opportunities for occupants, organizations, and legislatures the same.

At the core of Gigabit Urban areas is the arrangement of fast fiber-optic organizations. These organizations, constructed utilizing dainty glass or plastic strings to communicate information as beats of light, have the limit with regards to quick and proficient information move. While conventional broadband advances like Computerized Supporter Line (DSL) or link have served metropolitan regions for a really long time, they miss the mark in contrast with the capacities of fiber-optic organizations.

The benefits of Gigabit Urban communities are different. One of the most prompt advantages is the upgraded web insight for occupants. With gigabit-speed web, exercises like real time top quality recordings, web based gaming, and video conferencing become consistent and support free. This superior nature of administration not just fulfills the needs of present day computerized ways of life yet in addition opens up additional opportunities for schooling, diversion, and remote work.

Besides, Gigabit Urban communities assume a urgent part in cultivating monetary development and development. High velocity web goes about as an impetus for business venture and private company improvement, empowering quicker information moves, productive correspondence,

and admittance to cloud-based administrations. In a time where computerized network is inseparable from financial seriousness, urban communities with gigabit foundation are better situated to draw in organizations, speculation, and a talented labor force.

The meaning of Gigabit Urban communities reaches out past individual families and organizations. Metropolitan states can use fast availability to upgrade public administrations, execute savvy city drives, and work on in general metropolitan productivity. From savvy traffic the executives frameworks to smart garbage removal arrangements, the combination of gigabit-speed web permits urban communities to send state of the art advancements that upgrade the personal satisfaction for inhabitants.

The excursion toward Gigabit Urban communities is a multi-layered try that includes joint effort among public and confidential substances. Web access suppliers (ISPs) assume a focal part in sending the essential foundation, however metropolitan legislatures likewise contribute by establishing a helpful administrative climate and putting resources into the improvement of computerized framework. The public-private association model has demonstrated compelling in speeding up the rollout of gigabit organizations, with the two areas cooperating to connect the computerized partition.

As the idea of Gigabit Urban communities picks up speed, it is pivotal to consider the advancing scene of computerized availability. Past gigabit speeds, there is a developing accentuation on the improvement of organizations that can uphold considerably higher information move rates. The expression "past gigabit" epitomizes the following wilderness of availability, where velocities of 10 gigabits each second (10 Gbps) or more become the new norm.

Past gigabit network addresses a change in outlook in the computerized scene, with the possibility to reform how we collaborate with innovation. The coming of advancements, for example, 5G and the consistent development of fiber-optic organizations add to the acknowledgment of these remarkable velocities. The ramifications of such high velocity availability are immense and stretch out across different spaces, including medical care, training, diversion, and then some.

In the medical care area, the effect of past gigabit availability is extraordinary. Telemedicine, which has acquired conspicuousness lately, stands to benefit fundamentally from quicker and more solid web speeds. Top quality video discussions, continuous remote checking of patients, and the quick trade of clinical information become potential outcomes as well as real factors. Past gigabit network works with the consistent incorporation of innovation into medical services conveyance, upgrading patient consideration and further developing in general wellbeing results.

Training is another field where past gigabit availability can reclassify the opportunity for growth. The shift toward online schooling and e-learning stages has sped up, and high velocity web is an essential for a smooth and intelligent learning climate. Past gigabit speeds empower the conveyance of vivid instructive substance, support computer generated reality (VR) applications for upgraded growth opportunities, and work with cooperation among understudies and instructors across the globe.

Media outlets is no more peculiar to the effect of propelling availability. Past gigabit speeds introduce another period of superior grade, vivid substance conveyance. Web-based features can offer 4K as well as even 8K goal recordings without buffering, and augmented reality encounters become more consistent and similar. The capacity to download huge documents, for example, computer games or high-goal films, in practically no time further improves the shopper experience.

As urban areas embrace the potential outcomes of past gigabit availability, they position themselves at the cutting edge of mechanical advancement. The idea of shrewd urban communities, which influence information and availability to streamline metropolitan tasks, turns out to be more feasible with the sped up and unwavering quality gave by past gigabit organizations. From wise transportation frameworks to continuous ecological observing, urban communities can carry out a wide exhibit of savvy drives that improve manageability, effectiveness, and by and large decency.

The way to past gigabit availability includes tending to different difficulties and contemplations. Framework organization is a complex and asset escalated process that requires careful preparation and coordination. Beating actual boundaries, like troublesome landscape or existing framework impediments, requests creative arrangements and a guarantee to long haul arranging. Also, issues of reasonableness and computerized proficiency should be addressed to guarantee that the advantages of past gigabit network are open to all fragments of the populace.

Moreover, the security and protection ramifications of past gigabit network can't be neglected. As information move speeds increment, the volume of information being sent additionally develops dramatically. This flood of information requires powerful network safety measures to safeguard against expected dangers and breaks. Urban areas should put resources into secure and tough organizations, execute encryption conventions, and teach occupants and organizations about accepted procedures for online security.

In the domain of policymaking, states assume a urgent part in forming the direction of past gigabit network. Clear and ground breaking guidelines are fundamental to support private area interest in rapid framework.

Legislatures can likewise boost the advancement of inventive innovations and plans of action that help the development toward past gigabit speeds. Cooperation between states, confidential area partners, and the scholarly local area is crucial for making an all encompassing and reasonable structure for the computerized future.

The worldwide scene of past gigabit availability is assorted, with various locales advancing at different speeds. While certain urban communities are at the very front of sending gigabit and past gigabit framework, others face provokes in getting up to speed because of monetary requirements or geological impediments. Connecting the computerized partition requires purposeful endeavors from legislatures, industry players, and global associations to guarantee that each local area, no matter what its area or financial status, approaches rapid web.

All in all, the development from Gigabit Urban areas to past gigabit network addresses a dynamic and extraordinary excursion in the domain of metropolitan network. The sending of rapid web framework not just improves the computerized encounters of people and organizations yet in addition fills in as an impetus for monetary development, development, and the improvement of savvy urban communities. Past gigabit network opens up new outskirts in medical care, training, diversion, and different areas, introducing a period of extraordinary potential outcomes.

Nonetheless, the acknowledgment of past gigabit availability accompanies its portion of difficulties, from the intricacies of foundation arrangement to the basic of resolving issues connected with security, protection, and computerized consideration. State run administrations, industry partners, and networks should work cooperatively to explore these difficulties and guarantee that the advantages of fast availability are evenhandedly conveyed.

As we look toward the future, the vision of past gigabit network offers a brief look into a carefully interconnected reality where the potential for development exceeds all rational limitations. The excursion toward this future is an aggregate undertaking that requires key preparation, speculation, and a promise to building strong and comprehensive computerized biological systems. In embracing the open doors introduced by past gigabit availability, urban communities can situate themselves as centers of advancement, supportability, and success in the computerized age.

5.2 Impact of high-speed internet on urban development

The effect of high velocity web on metropolitan improvement is a multi-layered and groundbreaking power that has re-imagined the manner in which urban communities capability, develop, and collaborate with their occupants. As the computerized age keeps on unfurling, fast web has arisen as a basic empowering influence, forming the metropolitan scene in uncommon ways.

At the front of this change is the idea of Gigabit Urban communities, where far reaching admittance to gigabit-speed web has turned into a sign of moderate metropolitan turn of events. Gigabit-speed, characterized by information move paces of 1 gigabit each second (Gbps) or higher, has introduced another period of availability that goes past conventional broadband capacities. The organization of fast fiber-optic organizations, equipped for sending information at fantastic rates, lies at the core of this change in outlook.

One of the most prompt and recognizable effects of rapid web on metropolitan improvement is the upgraded personal satisfaction for inhabitants. Gigabit-speed web guarantees consistent and support free encounters for data transmission concentrated exercises like web based superior quality recordings, internet gaming, and video conferencing. This not just fulfills the needs of current advanced ways of life yet additionally opens up additional opportunities for diversion, instruction, and remote work.

The financial ramifications of fast web are similarly huge. Metropolitan regions with gigabit framework are better situated to cultivate financial development and advancement. High velocity web goes about as an impetus for business and private venture improvement, giving quicker information moves, proficient correspondence, and admittance to cloud-based administrations. In a time where computerized network is a vital determinant of financial seriousness, urban communities with strong fast framework are more appealing to organizations, financial backers, and a gifted labor force.

Besides, the effect of fast web reaches out past individual families and organizations to the domain of metropolitan administration. Regional authorities can use high velocity availability to upgrade public administrations, carry out savvy city drives, and work on generally speaking metropolitan effectiveness. From shrewd traffic the board frameworks to clever garbage removal arrangements, the joining of gigabit-speed web permits urban communities to send state of the art advances that upgrade the personal satisfaction for inhabitants while streamlining asset distribution.

The excursion toward Gigabit Urban communities is a cooperative exertion including both public and confidential substances. Web access suppliers (ISPs) assume a focal part in sending the vital foundation, while civil states contribute by establishing a favorable administrative climate and putting resources into computerized framework improvement. The progress of this organization model is obvious in the sped up rollout of gigabit organizations, restricting the computerized partition and guaranteeing that the advantages of high velocity web are open to a more extensive section of the populace.

As urban areas keep on embracing the conceivable outcomes of high velocity web, the idea of "past gigabit" network has arisen as the following wilderness. Past gigabit speeds, frequently surpassing 10 gigabits each second (10 Gbps), address a change in outlook in the computerized scene.

This development is worked with by innovations like 5G and the consistent headways in fiber-optic organizations, opening up exceptional potential outcomes across different spaces.

In the medical care area, the effect of past gigabit availability is groundbreaking. Telemedicine, which has seen huge development, stands to profit from quicker and more dependable web speeds. Superior quality video discussions, continuous far off persistent checking, and quick information trade become conceivable outcomes as well as fundamental parts of current medical services conveyance. Past gigabit network works with the consistent combination of innovation into medical services, upgrading patient consideration and further developing in general wellbeing results.

Schooling is another area where past gigabit network can reshape the growth opportunity. The flood in web-based schooling and e-learning stages requires high velocity web for a smooth and intuitive learning climate. Past gigabit speeds empower the conveyance of vivid instructive substance, support computer generated reality (VR) applications for improved opportunities for growth, and encourage joint effort among understudies and teachers on a worldwide scale.

Media outlets is no more interesting to the effect of propelling availability. Past gigabit speeds introduce another period of superior grade, vivid substance conveyance. Web-based features can offer 4K as well as even 8K goal recordings without buffering, and computer generated reality encounters become more consistent and similar. The capacity to download huge records, for example, computer games or high-goal motion pictures, in practically no time further upgrades the customer experience.

As urban communities embrace the potential outcomes of past gigabit availability, they position themselves at the front line of mechanical advancement. The acknowledgment of savvy urban areas, which influence information and availability to streamline metropolitan tasks, turns out to be more feasible with sped up and dependability. Wise transportation frameworks, ongoing natural observing, and a plenty of savvy drives improve maintainability, productivity, and by and large decency.

The way to past gigabit network includes tending to different difficulties and contemplations. Foundation sending is a complex and asset serious cycle requiring careful preparation and coordination. Defeating actual hindrances, like troublesome territory or existing framework constraints, requests creative arrangements and a promise to long haul arranging. Issues of moderateness and advanced proficiency should likewise be addressed to guarantee that the advantages of past gigabit availability are open to all portions of the populace.

Moreover, the security and protection ramifications of past gigabit network can't be disregarded. As information move speeds increment, the volume of information being communicated develops dramatically.

This convergence of information requires strong network safety measures to safeguard against likely dangers and breaks. Urban communities should put resources into secure and strong organizations, execute encryption conventions, and instruct occupants and organizations about accepted procedures for online security.

In the domain of policymaking, states assume a pivotal part in forming the direction of past gigabit network. Clear and ground breaking guidelines are fundamental to empower private area interest in rapid framework. States can boost the advancement of inventive innovations and plans of action that help the development toward past gigabit speeds. Joint effort between states, confidential area partners, and the scholarly local area is imperative for making an all encompassing and maintainable structure for the computerized future.

The worldwide scene of past gigabit network is assorted, with various areas advancing at different speeds. A few urban communities are at the front of sending gigabit and past gigabit framework, while others face provokes in getting up to speed because of financial requirements or geological constraints. Spanning the advanced gap requires coordinated endeavors from legislatures, industry players, and global associations to guarantee that each local area, no matter what its area or financial status, approaches rapid web.

Taking everything into account, the effect of rapid web on metropolitan improvement is significant and expansive. From the improved personal satisfaction for occupants to the monetary open doors for organizations and the extraordinary potential in areas like medical care and schooling, high velocity web has turned into a foundation of present day metropolitan living. As urban areas develop from Gigabit Urban areas to past gigabit network, they position themselves at the cutting edge of mechanical advancement, supportability, and thriving in the computerized age. The excursion toward rapid network is a dynamic and cooperative undertaking, requiring key preparation, venture, and a promise to building versatile and comprehensive computerized biological systems. Embracing the valuable open doors introduced by high velocity web, urban communities can shape a future where development exceeds all logical limitations, and the potential for development and improvement is boundless.

5.3 Technological advancements and innovations enabled by fiber optics

Mechanical progressions and advancements empowered by fiber optics have changed how data is sent, opening up additional opportunities across different ventures and altogether affecting the manner in which we impart, access data, and lead business. Fiber optics, which includes the transmission of information through slim strands of glass or plastic filaments utilizing beats of light, has shown to be a unique advantage in the realm of broadcast communications and then some.

One of the vital benefits of fiber optics lies in its capacity to send information at unimaginably high paces. Dissimilar to conventional copper-based links, which are restricted in transmission capacity and helpless to flag corruption over significant distances, fiber optics offer an answer that isn't just quicker yet in addition more solid. The utilization of light heartbeats considers the transmission of information at speeds moving toward the speed of light, pursuing fiber optics the favored decision for high velocity web associations and media communications organizations.

The effect of fiber optics on broadcast communications is especially significant. The organization of fiber-optic organizations has prepared for Gigabit Urban communities, where broad admittance to gigabit-speed web has turned into a reality. Gigabit-speed, portrayed by information move paces of 1 gigabit each second (Gbps) or higher, has changed the computerized scene, empowering consistent web based, superior quality video conferencing, and other data transfer capacity escalated applications.

Notwithstanding fast web, fiber optics play had an essential impact in the progression of media communications organizations, especially in the turn of events and sending of 5G innovation. 5G, the fifth era of versatile organizations, depends on a thick organization of little cells and high-recurrence groups for quicker information move rates and lower inactivity. Fiber-optic foundation gives the essential spine to help the rapid, low-inactivity necessities of 5G organizations, empowering the expansion of associated gadgets, savvy urban communities, and the Web of Things (IoT).

The Web of Things, specifically, has seen huge development and advancement because of the capacities of fiber optics. The consistent and rapid transmission of information worked with by fiber-optic organizations is instrumental in associating and dealing with the heap of gadgets that make up the IoT biological system. From shrewd homes and associated vehicles to modern robotization and medical care applications, fiber optics act as the hidden innovation that guarantees dependable and proficient correspondence between gadgets.

Also, the effect of fiber optics reaches out past broadcast communications to the domains of medical care and clinical innovation. In the field of telemedicine, fiber-optic organizations empower superior quality video discussions, far off quiet observing, and the quick trade of clinical information. This works on the openness of medical services administrations as well as upgrades the proficiency and adequacy of clinical finding and therapy.

The abilities of fiber optics have likewise added to the advancement of inventive clinical gadgets, like endoscopes and imaging frameworks. Fiber-optic sensors, equipped for communicating light through adaptable and dainty filaments, have become vital in clinical imaging, giving itemized visuals in negligibly obtrusive strategies. This works on the precision of clinical determinations as well as lessens the intrusiveness of specific clinical mediations.

In the domain of training, fiber optics play had a urgent impact in working with web based learning and e-learning stages. The fast and dependable web network given by fiber-optic organizations guarantee a consistent and intelligent growth opportunity. From video addresses and virtual study halls to cooperative internet based projects, fiber optics have turned into the foundation of computerized schooling, rising above geological obstructions and extending admittance to quality learning assets.

Media outlets, as well, has gone through a change empowered by fiber optics. Web-based features, offering top quality and, surprisingly, 4K or 8K goal recordings, depend on the rapid information transmission capacities of fiber-optic organizations. The consistent conveyance of content to purchasers, whether it be motion pictures, Television programs, or live occasions, has turned into a norm, reshaping customer assumptions and the plans of action of media outlets.

Besides, fiber optics have changed the manner in which organizations work and convey. Rapid and solid web associations are fundamental for everyday tasks, from leading video gatherings and teaming up on cloud-based stages to guaranteeing secure and productive information move. Fiber-optic organizations give the transmission capacity and dependability expected for organizations to flourish in an undeniably computerized and interconnected world.

In the monetary area, where the speed and security of information transmission are foremost, fiber optics have turned into a foundation of electronic exchanging and monetary exchanges. The low dormancy presented by fiber-optic associations is basic for high-recurrence exchanging, where parted second choices can have a huge effect. The monetary business' dependence on fiber optics highlights the innovation's job in working with constant information transmission and empowering worldwide monetary business sectors.

Also, the effect of fiber optics on metropolitan improvement couldn't possibly be more significant. Gigabit Urban communities, controlled by fiber-optic foundation, are better prepared to draw in organizations, cultivate advancement, and improve generally metropolitan proficiency. Savvy city drives, which influence information and network to streamline metropolitan activities, depend on the high velocity and solid web given by fiber optics. From keen transportation frameworks to energy the board and public security, fiber optics structure the foundation of shrewd urban communities, adding to economical and reasonable metropolitan conditions.

The arrangement of fiber optics, be that as it may, isn't without its difficulties. The forthright expenses of laying fiber-optic links and building the essential framework can be huge. Conquering these monetary hindrances frequently requires cooperation between government substances, confidential area partners, and broadcast communications suppliers. Also, resolving issues connected with option to proceed, administrative endorsements, and local area commitment is significant for the fruitful execution of fiber-optic tasks.

Besides, the security and protection ramifications of fiber optics need cautious thought. As the volume of information communicated through fiber-optic organizations increments, so does the significance of strong network safety measures. Encryption conventions, secure organization designs, and proactive danger location are fundamental parts of guaranteeing the uprightness and secrecy of information sent through fiber optics.

Looking forward, the continuous development of fiber optics keeps on molding the innovative scene. Past gigabit network, there is a developing accentuation on stretching the boundaries of information move rates. The idea of "past gigabit" embodies the following outskirts, where paces surpassing 10 gigabits each second (10 Gbps) become the new norm. This advancement is driven by progressions in fiber-optic innovation, including the improvement of new materials and methods that push the limits of information transmission.

All in all, mechanical progressions and developments empowered by fiber optics significantly affect the manner in which we convey, access data, and lead business. From fast web and media communications organizations to medical services, schooling, and metropolitan turn of events, fiber optics have turned into a central empowering influence of progress in the computerized age. As the world keeps on embracing the capacities of fiber-optic innovation, the potential for additional development and change across different areas stays boundless, introducing a future where network exceeds all logical limitations.

5.4 Global examples of cities leading the way in high-speed connectivity

Rapid network has turned into a basic driver of metropolitan turn of events and monetary development, with urban communities all over the planet contending to set up a good foundation for themselves as pioneers in the computerized age. The journey for rapid web isn't just about quicker downloads and smoother streaming; it's tied in with situating urban communities as centers of development, drawing in organizations, cultivating business, and upgrading the general personal satisfaction for occupants. In this worldwide scene, a few urban communities stand apart as praiseworthy models, displaying the extraordinary effect of fast network across different spaces.

Seoul, South Korea: A Trailblazer in Gigabit Web

South Korea has for quite some time been perceived as a worldwide innovator in broadband and rapid web reception. Seoul, its capital, has arisen as a trailblazer in the organization of gigabit web, furnishing occupants with admittance to web rates of up to 10 gigabits each second (Gbps). The city's obligation to building a vigorous computerized foundation has situated it as a testbed for state of the art innovations and shrewd city drives.

Seoul's progress in fast network can be credited to the public authority's essential ventures and coordinated efforts with private area elements. The city's far reaching broadband arrangement, sent off in the mid 2000s, meant to give reasonable and high velocity web admittance to each family. The outcome is a city where occupants partake in probably the quickest and most dependable web associations universally.

Past giving quick web to homes, Seoul's rapid network fills in as the spine for different brilliant city drives. The coordination of innovation into metropolitan activities incorporates savvy transportation frameworks, shrewd energy the executives, and information driven administration. These drives add to a more productive, supportable, and decent metropolitan climate.

Singapore: A Shrewd Country Driven by Fiber Optics

Singapore, frequently alluded to as a "Shrewd Country," has situated itself as a worldwide forerunner in utilizing fast network for extensive metropolitan turn of events. The city-state's prosperity is supported by its broad fiber-optic framework, furnishing organizations and inhabitants with rapid web access.

Singapore's excursion towards turning into a Brilliant Country started with the improvement of its Cutting edge Cross country Broadband Organization (NGNBN). This drive meant to give unavoidable super fast broadband admittance to all families, organizations, and government offices. The NGNBN, based on fiber-optic innovation, has been instrumental in empowering gigabit-speed web and supporting a large number of computerized administrations.

The effect of rapid availability in Singapore goes past web access. The city-state has executed drives like Shrewd Homes, Savvy Structures, and Brilliant Networks, all fueled by fast fiber optics. The combination of sensors, information examination, and availability has upgraded proficiency in energy utilization, squander the executives, and metropolitan portability. Singapore's methodology fills in as an outline for different urban communities seeking to embrace the potential outcomes of rapid network in building brilliant and feasible metropolitan conditions.

Stockholm, Sweden: A Center point for Development

Stockholm has procured its standing as an educated city and a center point for development, driven to a limited extent by its obligation to fast web. The city's emphasis on computerized framework has drawn in tech new businesses, worldwide companies, and a profoundly talented labor force, adding to its status as a main worldwide tech center point.

Sweden's initial interests in fiber-optic organizations established the groundwork for Stockholm's rapid network. The city's broad fiber-optic foundation upholds quick web as well as works with the advancement of tech-concentrated businesses, like gaming, programming improvement, and biotechnology.

Stockholm's accomplishments in fast network are entwined with its accentuation on computerized proficiency and schooling. The city has sustained a culture of development and business venture, with drives like cooperating spaces, hatcheries, and joint effort centers. This environment, upheld by fast web, has led to effective new businesses and drawn in significant tech organizations, supporting Stockholm's situation as a worldwide development place.

Hong Kong: The Asian Monetary Center

Hong Kong, a worldwide monetary center, has embraced rapid network as a foundation of its financial seriousness. The city's essential interests in fiber-optic foundation have not just furnished occupants with the absolute quickest web speeds all around the world however have likewise upheld the monetary business' requirement for fast and secure information transmission.

Hong Kong's progress in fast availability is apparent in its broad admittance to gigabit-speed web and the arrangement of cutting edge versatile organizations, including 5G. The monetary area, where parted second choices can influence market results, depends on the low dormancy and high unwavering quality presented by fiber optics.

In addition, Hong Kong's way to deal with fast availability reaches out past money. The city's obligation to savvy city drives incorporates the sending of IoT gadgets for ecological checking, wise transportation frameworks, and energy-proficient structures. These endeavors exhibit how fast network can add to the general flexibility and manageability of a worldwide city.

Chattanooga, USA: Civil Broadband Example of overcoming adversity

Chattanooga, a fair sized city in Tennessee, USA, has turned into an image of civil broadband achievement, showing the extraordinary force of local area driven high velocity network drives. The city's Electric Power Board (EPB) set out on an aggressive undertaking to construct a far reaching fiber-optic organization, giving inhabitants admittance to gigabit-speed web.

Chattanooga's choice to put resources into civil broadband was driven by a longing to renew the neighborhood economy and upgrade occupants' personal satisfaction. The subsequent Gigabit City drive not just followed through on its commitment of quick web yet in addition pulled in organizations, business visionaries, and tech ability to the city.

The effect of rapid network in Chattanooga goes past the computerized domain. The city has seen financial renewal, with the improvement of a flourishing tech area and expanded open positions. Chattanooga's example of overcoming adversity features the potential for networks to assume command over their computerized future and utilize rapid web as an impetus for nearby turn of events.

Tokyo, Japan: Availability for All

Tokyo, one of the world's most crowded and innovatively progressed urban communities, has focused on general admittance to fast web as a crucial part of its metropolitan turn of events. The city's obligation to network stretches out to its vision of making a comprehensive computerized society, guaranteeing that all inhabitants approach the advantages of rapid web.

Japan's broad fiber-optic organizations give Tokyo the foundation expected to convey quick and solid web to its inhabitants. The city's way to deal with high velocity network incorporates drives to connect the computerized partition, guaranteeing that even underserved networks approach gigabit-speed web.

Tokyo's rapid availability isn't restricted to homes; it saturates different parts of metropolitan life. The city's productive public transportation frameworks, savvy foundation, and computerized administrations depend on vigorous availability to upgrade the general personal satisfaction for occupants. Tokyo's obligation to widespread admittance to rapid web features the potential for innovation to be a power for social incorporation and fair metropolitan turn of events.

Barcelona, Spain: A Forerunner in Shrewd City Development

Barcelona has procured praise as a forerunner in brilliant city development, utilizing fast network to upgrade metropolitan living and address the difficulties of present day urbanization. The city's obligation to building a savvy city biological system is clear in its far reaching utilization of innovation, information, and network to work on metropolitan administrations and maintainability.

Barcelona's broad fiber-optic framework shapes the foundation of its savvy city drives. The city's execution of IoT gadgets, sensors, and information examination adds to insightful transportation frameworks, squander the executives, and energy proficiency. These drives, controlled by rapid web, have worked on the effectiveness of metropolitan tasks as well as made a more manageable and reasonable metropolitan climate.

Besides, Barcelona's accentuation on resident commitment and advanced incorporation separates it. The city's obligation to involving innovation to support its inhabitants incorporates drives to connect the computerized partition and guarantee that all residents approach the open doors managed the cost of by high velocity availability. Barcelona's all encompassing way to deal with brilliant city improvement fills in as a motivation for other metropolitan communities looking to saddle the capability of rapid web for complete metropolitan advancement.

Shenzhen, China: From Assembling Center point to Development Center

Shenzhen, when referred to fundamentally as an assembling center point, has changed into a worldwide development place, and rapid network plays had an essential impact in this transformation. The city's fast improvement as an innovation and development center point is intently attached to its obligation to building progressed computerized framework.

China's interests in 5G innovation, combined with Shenzhen's broad fiber-optic organizations, have established a climate helpful for development and business venture. The city's flourishing tech environment, home to various new companies and innovation goliaths, benefits from fast web that empowers quick information move, coordinated effort, and the improvement of state of the art advancements.

6

Chapter 6

Fiber Optics in Emerging Technologies

Fiber optics, an innovation that bridles the transmission of data through beats of light along strands of glass or plastic, has arisen as a foundation in the domain of present day broadcast communications and data innovation. Its unrivaled capacity to communicate information at fantastic rates over significant distances with negligible sign misfortune has situated fiber optics as a critical empowering influence for a plenty of arising innovations.

One of the essential benefits of fiber optics lies in its ability for fast information transmission. Customary copper-based links, utilized in more seasoned correspondence frameworks, battle to stay up with the rising requests for data transfer capacity. Fiber optic links, then again, communicate information utilizing light signals, considering quicker information move rates. This is especially fundamental in the time of top quality video web based, web based gaming, and the steadily growing domain of the Web of Things (IoT), where huge measures of information should be communicated consistently and rapidly.

The usage of fiber optics stretches out past customary information transmission. The clinical field, for example, has embraced fiber optic innovation for different applications. Fiber optic sensors empower exact and constant checking of essential signs in patients, giving medical care experts precise information for opportune mediations. Moreover, fiber optic imaging methods, like endoscopy, have altered clinical diagnostics by offering high-goal imaging with negligible intrusiveness.

As the interest for rapid web keeps on raising, fiber optics is progressively turning into the foundation of broadband organizations. The organization of fiber-to-the-home (FTTH) and fiber-to-the-premises (FTTP) advancements has changed web network by conveying gigabit-speed web straightforwardly to homes and organizations. This progress from conventional copper-based foundation to fiber optics guarantees a hearty and future-confirmation network equipped for meeting the consistently developing information requests of the computerized age.

With regards to 5G innovation, fiber optics assumes a critical part in giving the important foundation to help the organization of super quick and low-idleness organizations. The remarkable rates guaranteed by 5G organizations depend vigorously on the accessibility of high-limit fiber optic associations.

The organization of little cells, fundamental for the densification of 5G organizations, requires a thick fiber optic foundation to guarantee proficient network and ideal execution.

The energy area has likewise seen the coordination of fiber optics into its tasks. Fiber optic sensors are utilized for primary wellbeing observing of basic framework, like scaffolds and pipelines. These sensors can recognize minute changes in strain, temperature, and different boundaries, giving early admonitions of likely issues and adding to the general security and unwavering quality of framework frameworks.

Moreover, the utilization of fiber optics in the oil and gas industry has demonstrated instrumental in downhole detecting and checking. Fiber optic sensors sent in oil wells can gauge boundaries like temperature and strain continuously, empowering administrators to streamline creation and upgrade supply the executives. The strength of fiber optics in brutal conditions makes them appropriate for such requesting applications.

In the domain of transportation, fiber optic innovation is assuming a groundbreaking part in the improvement of savvy urban communities and clever transportation frameworks. Fiber optic organizations support the correspondence foundation for traffic the executives, reconnaissance frameworks, and other savvy city applications. High velocity and solid availability given by fiber optics is necessary to the outcome of associated and independent vehicles, working with continuous correspondence among vehicles and foundation for upgraded security and effectiveness.

The utilization of fiber optics reaches out past the limits of our planet. In space investigation, fiber optics is utilized for fast correspondence among rocket and ground stations. The tremendous distances engaged with space missions require a dependable and proficient method for sending information, and fiber optics offer an answer that is both lightweight and prepared to do high information move rates.

The organization of fiber optics in arising advancements isn't restricted to Earth and space. Submerged correspondence frameworks influence fiber optic links for communicating information across maritime regions. The high transmission capacity and low sign misfortune attributes of fiber optics make them ideal for keeping up with solid correspondence joins in testing submerged conditions. This is vital for applications like seaward penetrating, natural checking, and submarine link frameworks.

As the world changes towards sustainable power sources, fiber optics is assuming a urgent part in the progression of sun oriented energy advances. Fiber optic sensors are used for observing the presentation of sunlight based chargers, giving continuous information on temperature, strain, and different boundaries. This information empowers administrators to streamline the effectiveness of sunlight based power frameworks and address issues immediately, adding to the general dependability and supportability of sustainable power foundation.

The combination of fiber optics into arising advances isn't without its difficulties. One huge impediment is the underlying expense related with the organization of fiber optic framework. While the drawn out benefits are significant, the forthright speculation can be an obstruction for certain businesses and districts. Nonetheless, continuous headways in fiber optic assembling and establishment innovations are steadily decreasing these expenses, making fiber optics a more open and feasible choice for different applications.

One more test lies in the similarity of existing frameworks with fiber optic innovation. Redesigning foundation to oblige fiber optics might require critical changes, particularly in areas where heritage frameworks are profoundly settled in. The consistent coordination of fiber optics frequently requires an extensive redesign of the current foundation, which can be a complex and tedious interaction.

In spite of these difficulties, the benefits presented by fiber optics regarding pace, unwavering quality, and information limit offset the underlying obstacles. The continuous innovative work in fiber optic innovation are tending to these difficulties, preparing for more extensive reception across different ventures.

Looking forward, the development of fiber optics is ready to assume a pivotal part in forming the fate of arising advances. One area of critical commitment is quantum correspondence, where fiber optics can work with the transmission of quantum data for secure and unhackable correspondence. Quantum key circulation (QKD) frameworks, depending on the standards of quantum mechanics, use fiber optics to send cryptographic keys safely, offering another boondocks in secure correspondence.

The idea of "brilliant urban communities" is one more area where fiber optics is set to make a permanent imprint. The interconnectivity of different metropolitan frameworks, like transportation, energy, and public administrations, depends on hearty and rapid correspondence organizations. Fiber optics, with its capacity to deal with huge volumes of information with negligible idleness, is a foundation for incorporating the framework expected to change urban communities into smart, proficient, and reasonable environments.

In the domain of man-made reasoning (artificial intelligence) and AI, the job of fiber optics is turning out to be progressively huge. The preparation and activity of simulated intelligence models frequently include tremendous measures of information that should be handled and communicated quickly. Fiber optic organizations, with their high transfer speed and low dormancy, give the spine to supporting the computational requests of simulated intelligence, empowering the consistent coordination of AI applications in different enterprises.

The coming of increased reality (AR) and computer generated reality (VR) is one more outskirts where fiber optics is making significant commitments. These vivid innovations require fast and low-inactivity associations with convey a consistent and practical experience to clients.

Fiber optics, with its capacity to communicate a lot of information at high rates, guarantees that AR and VR applications can work without slack, furnishing clients with a vivid and responsive experience.

All in all, the job of fiber optics in arising advancements is diverse and keeps on extending across different enterprises. From upsetting correspondence organizations and medical services frameworks to empowering progressions in space investigation and environmentally friendly power, fiber optics has turned into a crucial innovation in the advanced time. As continuous innovative work push the limits of what is conceivable with fiber optics, the potential for its incorporation into future advances stays boundless. As we stand on the cusp of another mechanical time, the light-directing capacities of fiber optics enlighten the way ahead, directing us towards a future where network, speed, and dependability are principal.

6.1 Role of fiber optics in supporting emerging technologies (5G, IoT, etc.)

Fiber optics, with its capacity to communicate information utilizing beats of light, has arisen as a key part in supporting and catalyzing the development of different arising innovations. Among these, 5G and the Web of Things (IoT) stand apart as especially extraordinary, and the job of fiber optics in supporting their abilities is crucial.

The organization of 5G organizations addresses a change in outlook in remote correspondence, promising exceptional speed, low idleness, and enormous network. Fiber optics plays a fundamental job in understanding the maximum capacity of 5G innovation. The high-recurrence signals utilized in 5G organizations, particularly in the millimeter-wave groups, are all the more successfully communicated through fiber optic links, guaranteeing negligible sign misfortune and empowering the high information move rates that portray 5G.

Fiber optics, related to 5G, addresses the unquenchable interest for quicker and more dependable web network. The customary copper-based foundation battles to stay up with the blossoming information necessities of present day applications, from top quality video real time to expanded reality. Fiber optics not just gives the essential transfer speed to 5G organizations yet additionally works with the arrangement of little cells, which are urgent for accomplishing the high organization thickness expected for 5G.

The mix of fiber optics and 5G likewise proclaims another time in the Web of Things. IoT, described by the interconnection of gadgets that can convey and share information, depends on vigorous and rapid organizations. Fiber optics, with its capacity to deal with huge volumes of information and give low-inertness correspondence, turns into the foundation of the IoT biological system. From shrewd homes and urban communities to modern IoT applications, the dependability and speed of fiber optics are essential for consistent availability and constant information trade.

In the medical care area, the cooperative energy between fiber optics and IoT is reshaping patient consideration and clinical diagnostics. Wearable gadgets outfitted with sensors can constantly screen crucial signs and communicate continuous information to medical services suppliers. Fiber optic organizations guarantee the quick and dependable transmission of this information, empowering medical care experts to screen patients from a distance and mediate expeditiously when vital.

Also, in brilliant urban areas, where interconnected frameworks improve metropolitan residing, fiber optics coordinated with IoT innovation empowers effective traffic the executives, natural observing, and public administrations. The ongoing information created by IoT gadgets is flawlessly communicated through fiber optic organizations, supporting the interconnectedness of different frameworks and adding to the general maintainability and usefulness of shrewd urban communities.

Past 5G and IoT, fiber optics likewise assumes a vital part in reshaping the scene of server farms. The remarkable development of information in the computerized age requests superior execution information capacity and handling offices. Fiber optic associations inside and between server farms empower quick information move, lessening inactivity and improving by and large execution. As distributed computing turns out to be progressively essential to different ventures, the productivity of fiber optics becomes central in supporting the requests of information escalated applications and administrations.

In the energy area, fiber optics is instrumental in the organization of brilliant networks. Savvy matrices influence progressed correspondence and control advances to upgrade the dependability and proficiency of electrical frameworks. Fiber optic organizations give the vital correspondence framework to constant checking and control of the lattice, empowering utilities to answer quickly to vacillations popular and advance the circulation of power.

Moreover, fiber optics tracks down applications in the field of remote detecting and observing. Fiber optic sensors can be conveyed in different conditions, from modern settings to basic foundation, for checking boundaries like temperature, tension, and strain. These sensors give constant information, taking into consideration early discovery of peculiarities and expected issues. In the oil and gas industry, for instance, fiber optic sensors are utilized in downhole applications to screen well circumstances and advance creation processes.

In the aviation and safeguard area, the lightweight and elite presentation attributes of fiber optics settle on it an optimal decision for correspondence frameworks in airplane and space apparatus. Fiber optic links offer a dependable and secure method for communicating information over significant distances, defeating the impediments of customary copper links. In space investigation missions, where correspondence is significant for communicating logical information and keeping in touch with shuttle, fiber optics add to the achievement and proficiency of the mission.

Also, the coordination of fiber optics in arising advances stretches out to ecological checking and logical exploration. Submerged fiber optic links, for example, work with the transmission of information from remote ocean sensors to investigate vessels, adding to how we might interpret maritime biological systems. The solidness and high data transmission of fiber optics make them appropriate for unforgiving conditions, guaranteeing dependable correspondence in testing conditions.

With regards to sustainable power, fiber optic sensors assume a pivotal part in checking the presentation of sunlight based chargers and wind turbines. These sensors can give continuous information on boundaries like temperature, strain, and vibration, permitting administrators to streamline the proficiency of environmentally friendly power frameworks. The reconciliation of fiber optics in environmentally friendly power framework adds to the general unwavering quality and maintainability of these frameworks.

While the job of fiber optics in supporting arising advances is clear, difficulties and contemplations go with its broad reception. One remarkable test is the underlying expense related with conveying fiber optic framework. The establishment of fiber optic links requires huge speculation, and the expense can be an impediment for ventures or districts with restricted monetary assets. Be that as it may, the drawn out benefits, including higher information move speeds and decreased upkeep costs, frequently legitimize the forthright speculation.

Another thought is the requirement for a far reaching and very much arranged change from existing copper-based foundation to fiber optics. This change requires cautious reconciliation into existing frameworks, and at times, a total upgrade of foundation might be vital. Similarity issues with heritage frameworks and the requirement for gifted faculty to deal with fiber optic establishments are factors that associations should address during the progress interaction.

Moreover, the issue of safety in fiber optic organizations can't be ignored. While fiber optics give a solid medium to information transmission, they are not insusceptible to potential digital dangers. Associations should execute strong network protection measures to safeguard delicate information communicated through fiber optic organizations, particularly in basic areas like medical care, money, and guard.

In spite of these difficulties, the benefits presented by fiber optics in supporting arising advancements offset the impediments. Continuous innovative work endeavors keep on tending to cost-related concerns and work on the productivity of fiber optic frameworks. The developing scene of media communications and data innovation further accentuates the requirement for solid and elite execution organizations, making fiber optics an undeniably fundamental part of current framework.

Looking forward, the job of fiber optics in supporting arising advancements is set to extend much further. Quantum correspondence, an expanding field that use the standards of quantum mechanics for secure correspondence, holds guarantee for the eventual fate of fiber optics. Quantum key dissemination (QKD) frameworks, which use fiber optics to send cryptographic keys safely, address another outskirts in guaranteeing the honesty and classification of correspondence channels.

Man-made brainpower (computer based intelligence) and AI (ML) are likewise regions where the job of fiber optics is probably going to turn out to be more articulated. The preparation and activity of simulated intelligence and ML models include the quick handling of immense measures of information, and fiber optic organizations give the important foundation to help these computational requests. As computer based intelligence and ML applications become progressively coordinated into different enterprises, the dependence on fiber optics for proficient information move and correspondence will keep on developing.

Expanded reality (AR) and augmented reality (VR), vivid advances that request high velocity and low-inactivity associations, are ready to profit from the abilities of fiber optics. The consistent transmission of huge volumes of information expected for AR and VR encounters is made conceivable by fiber optic organizations. As these advances become more common in regions like gaming, schooling, and preparing, the job of fiber optics in conveying a responsive and vivid client experience turns out to be progressively huge.

6.2 Future applications and possibilities

The future applications and conceivable outcomes of fiber optics are tremendous and dynamic, promising to reshape businesses and improve innovative abilities across different spaces. As the world keeps on propelling, the incorporation of fiber optics into arising advancements opens ways to new open doors and changes.

One of the promising boondocks for the eventual fate of fiber optics lies in quantum correspondence. Quantum correspondence use the standards of quantum mechanics to get correspondence channels, giving a degree of safety that is hypothetically strong. Fiber optics, with its capacity to communicate light signals with negligible misfortune, turns into an essential part in the sending of quantum key dispersion (QKD) frameworks. QKD frameworks use fiber optics to send cryptographic keys safely, offering a quantum-secure technique for scrambling correspondence channels. As network safety turns into an undeniably basic worry in the computerized age, the turn of events and execution of quantum correspondence advances utilizing fiber optics address a change in perspective in guaranteeing the uprightness and classification of touchy data.

Man-made reasoning (artificial intelligence) and AI (ML) are at the cutting edge of mechanical headways, driving development across enterprises. Fiber optics assumes an essential part in supporting the computational requests of computer based intelligence and ML applications. The quick transmission of enormous datasets between handling units is fundamental for preparing and working man-made intelligence models actually. Fiber optic organizations give the high transfer speed and low idleness expected to work with the consistent progression of information, empowering the proficient sending of simulated intelligence and ML advancements.

As these advancements proceed to develop and find applications in different fields like medical care, finance, and independent frameworks, the dependence on fiber optics as a major foundation part will develop.

Increased reality (AR) and computer generated reality (VR) are vivid advances that can possibly upset how we communicate with the advanced world. Fiber optics, with its capacity to communicate enormous volumes of information at high velocities, is vital to conveying a responsive and sensible AR and VR experience. The low idleness given by fiber optic organizations guarantees that clients can connect with virtual conditions progressively, improving the general nature of AR and VR applications. As these advances become more common in gaming, training, medical care, and different areas, the job of fiber optics in empowering consistent and vivid encounters will turn out to be progressively conspicuous.

The advancement of savvy urban areas is intently attached to the abilities of fiber optics. As metropolitan populaces keep on developing, the requirement for proficient and interconnected frameworks becomes fundamental. Fiber optics, joined with the Web of Things (IoT), fills in as the spine for the advancement of shrewd urban areas. The coordination of sensors, cameras, and other IoT gadgets into metropolitan framework creates immense measures of information that should be sent and handled progressively. Fiber optic organizations give the important rapid and dependable availability to help these interconnected frameworks, working with brilliant transportation, energy the board, garbage removal, and public administrations. The eventual fate of shrewd urban areas depends on the proceeded with headway of fiber optic advances to fulfill the steadily expanding needs for network and information move.

In the field of medical care, the future uses of fiber optics hold the possibility to change diagnostics and therapy. Fiber optic sensors, with their capacity to gauge different boundaries, can be used for ongoing checking of patients and basic clinical hardware. Wearable gadgets integrating fiber optic sensors can give ceaseless and harmless checking of imperative signs, permitting medical care experts to assemble precise information for opportune intercessions. Fiber optic imaging methods, like endoscopy, are probably going to see further headways, empowering high-goal and negligibly intrusive operations. The incorporation of fiber optics into clinical advances adds to the improvement of telemedicine and far off understanding observing, upgrading admittance to medical care administrations.

Environmentally friendly power foundation stands to profit from the proceeded with coordination of fiber optics. The observing and improvement of sunlight based chargers, wind turbines, and other environmentally friendly power frameworks depend on constant information on different boundaries. Fiber optic sensors, fit for enduring cruel ecological circumstances, give a way to productively gather this information. As the world changes toward feasible energy sources, the job of fiber optics in guaranteeing the dependability and execution of sustainable power framework turns out to be progressively basic.

The investigation of space is a region where fiber optics is ready to assume a huge part from here on out. Space missions, whether automated or monitored, require solid correspondence frameworks for sending information among shuttle and ground stations. Fiber optic innovation offers a lightweight and superior exhibition answer for space correspondence, guaranteeing the productive exchange of logical information, pictures, and telemetry. As humankind looks toward aggressive missions to the Moon, Mars, and then some, fiber optics will be a key empowering agent in laying out hearty correspondence joins over huge distances in the unforgiving climate of room.

In the domain of submerged investigation, fiber optics opens up opportunities for headways in oceanography and marine examination. Submerged fiber optic links can send information from remote ocean sensors to investigate vessels, giving bits of knowledge into maritime environments, geographical highlights, and environment designs. The high transfer speed and low sign misfortune qualities of fiber optics make them appropriate for keeping up with solid correspondence joins in testing submerged conditions. This ability is urgent for applications like ecological checking, seaward boring, and the foundation of submerged observatories.

The potential for fiber optics stretches out to the democratization of admittance to high velocity web. In many regions of the planet, especially in country and distant regions, there is a computerized partition because of the absence of solid network. The future sending of fiber-to-the-home (FTTH) and fiber-to-the-premises (FTTP) advances expects to overcome this issue by bringing high velocity web straightforwardly to homes and organizations. As headways in fiber optic assembling and establishment innovations proceed, the expense of conveying fiber optic framework is probably going to diminish, making it a more open and reasonable choice for growing web access worldwide.

The incorporation of fiber optics into transportation frameworks holds the commitment of improving security, proficiency, and supportability. In the period of associated and independent vehicles, fiber optic organizations give the correspondence framework to continuous information trade among vehicles and foundation. This network is fundamental for empowering elements like vehicle-to-vehicle (V2V) correspondence, traffic the executives, and independent route. Fiber optics add to the advancement of clever transportation frameworks, where vehicles can speak with one another and with foundation components to streamline traffic stream, lessen blockage, and improve generally security.

In the modern area, the reception of Industry 4.0 standards is driving the coordination of fiber optics for savvy fabricating. Fiber optic sensors can be sent in assembling cycles to screen boundaries like temperature, strain, and vibration continuously. This information empowers prescient support, enhancing hardware execution and limiting margin time. The rapid information move capacities of fiber optics support the effective trade of data between machines, adding to the mechanization and availability of savvy manufacturing plants.

Notwithstanding the heap prospects and promising applications, challenges persevere in the far and wide reception of fiber optics. The underlying expense of sending fiber optic foundation stays a huge obstruction for certain enterprises and locales. Nonetheless, continuous innovative work endeavors intend to address this test, zeroing in on diminishing the expense of fiber optic parts and establishment processes. Moreover, the requirement for talented staff to deal with fiber optic establishments and upkeep highlights the significance of putting resources into preparing projects to construct a labor force fit for supporting the developing interest for fiber optic innovations.

The security of fiber optic organizations is one more area of continuous concern. As information sent through fiber optics turns out to be progressively basic and delicate, guaranteeing the respectability and classification of correspondence channels is vital. Associations and scientists are effectively creating encryption techniques and network safety measures to safeguard against likely dangers to fiber optic organizations.

All in all, the future applications and potential outcomes of fiber optics length a different scope of businesses and innovations, forming the direction of development and network. From quantum correspondence and man-made reasoning to shrewd urban communities, medical services, and space investigation, fiber optics arises as a flexible and crucial innovation. As innovative work endeavors keep on propelling the capacities of fiber optics and address existing difficulties, the potential for extraordinary effect on the manner in which we impart, investigate, and cooperate with our reality is monstrous. The development of fiber optics isn't simply an innovative progression; it is an excursion toward a future where network, speed, and unwavering quality rethink the limits of what is conceivable.

6.3 Collaboration between fiber optic technology and other cutting-edge innovations

The eventual fate of fiber optics is obviously encouraging, yet with the fast development of innovation and the rising reconciliation of fiber optics into different areas, a bunch of likely difficulties and contemplations arise that require cautious consideration and vital preparation. Exploring these difficulties will be significant in guaranteeing the proceeded with progress and manageability of fiber optic advancements in the years to come.

One of the preeminent difficulties lies in the domain of network protection. As the volume of information communicated through fiber optic organizations keeps on taking off, the significance of getting these organizations against digital dangers becomes fundamental. Cybercriminals might take advantage of weaknesses in fiber optic frameworks to acquire unapproved admittance to delicate data or upset basic administrations. Creating vigorous encryption techniques, carrying out secure organization designs, and remaining in front of arising digital dangers are basic for shielding the uprightness and classification of information sent through fiber optics.

Besides, the dependence on fiber optics in basic areas like medical care, money, and protection highlights the meaning of network safety. Medical services frameworks, for example, progressively influence fiber optic organizations for sending delicate patient information and empowering telemedicine. The expected split the difference of such information presents huge dangers to patient security and the general honesty of medical care administrations. Essentially, monetary foundations depend on fiber optics for fast and secure exchanges, making them expected focuses for digital assaults. A proactive and cooperative methodology among partners, including industry players, administrative bodies, and online protection specialists, is fundamental to relieve these dangers and guarantee the flexibility of fiber optic organizations.

The continuous change from customary copper-based framework to fiber optics presents an extensive test regarding cost. The forthright speculation expected for conveying fiber optic links, particularly in locales or ventures with restricted monetary assets, can be a boundary to reception. While the drawn out benefits, including higher information move speeds and decreased upkeep costs, legitimize the underlying venture, there is a requirement for inventive funding models and motivators to work with the far and wide organization of fiber optics. Legislatures, industry players, and worldwide associations might assume a significant part in tending to this test through drives that advance the moderateness and openness of fiber optic advances.

Similarity issues with existing framework address one more thought later on reception of fiber optics. Updating heritage frameworks to oblige fiber optics might require huge changes and, at times, a total redesign of existing foundation. Enterprises that vigorously depend on laid out advances and frameworks might confront interruptions during the progress, prompting possible personal time and efficiency misfortunes. Vital preparation, staged execution, and cooperation between partners are fundamental to guarantee a smooth combination of fiber optics into different areas without compromising functional congruity.

The lack of gifted staff with mastery in fiber optics is a test that could block the consistent reception and upkeep of fiber optic organizations. Introducing and keeping up with fiber optic foundation requires particular information and preparing. The interest for gifted specialists, architects, and organization chairmen capable in fiber optics is probably going to increment with the developing sending of this innovation. Instructive organizations, in a joint effort with industry partners, should foster projects that outfit people with the fundamental abilities to configuration, introduce, and keep up with fiber optic organizations. Labor force improvement drives and apprenticeship projects can assume a crucial part in tending to the deficiency of talented experts in the field of fiber optics.

Natural contemplations are acquiring unmistakable quality in the talk encompassing innovation and framework improvement. While fiber optics themselves are harmless to the ecosystem contrasted with conventional copper links, the assembling and removal of fiber optic parts have related ecological effects. The creation of optical strands and related materials includes energy utilization and unrefined substance extraction. Moreover, the removal of obsolete or harmed fiber optic links might present natural difficulties. The business must proactively investigate feasible practices in fiber optic assembling, reusing programs, and naturally cognizant removal strategies to limit its biological impression.

The issue of option to proceed and the administrative structure encompassing the establishment of fiber optic framework is one more thought for what's in store. Getting the fundamental consents and exploring administrative cycles can be tedious and complex. States and administrative bodies assume a vital part in smoothing out these cycles, guaranteeing that the sending of fiber optic organizations lines up with metropolitan preparation and ecological guidelines. Coordinated effort between general society and confidential areas is crucial for address administrative difficulties and work with the effective development of fiber optic foundation.

As the interest for higher information move speeds keeps on rising, the impediments forced by the material science of light transmission through fiber optics become a thought for what's in store. While fiber optics presently offer unrivaled speed and data transmission, there are intrinsic limits connected with signal misfortune over significant distances. Innovative work endeavors are in progress to address these impediments through developments like enhancement advancements and sign recovery. Proceeded with interest in propelling the capacities of fiber optic frameworks will be urgent to fulfill the steadily developing needs for quicker and more dependable correspondence.

One more thought for the eventual fate of fiber optics spins around the potential for signal obstruction and weakening. Outside variables like curves, turns, or natural circumstances can affect the transmission of light signals through fiber optic links. Understanding and relieving these issues are fundamental to keeping up with signal trustworthiness and guaranteeing predictable execution. Continuous examination into materials and plans that limit signal weakening, combined with vigorous establishment rehearses, is basic for tending to these difficulties.

Moreover, the fate of fiber optics is complicatedly connected to the continuous advancements in remote correspondence innovations. While fiber optics give unmatched speed and unwavering quality, the development of remote advancements, especially with regards to 6G and then some, may introduce elective answers for specific applications. Adjusting the qualities of fiber optics with the benefits presented by remote correspondence will require a nuanced way to deal with network plan and foundation arranging. Half breed arrangements that join fiber optics with cutting edge remote innovations might arise as the need might arise.

The potential for interruptions brought about by cataclysmic events or mishaps represents a huge test for the eventual fate of fiber optics. The actual weakness of fiber optic links to occasions like seismic tremors, floods, or development exercises requires strong making arrangements for network strength and overt repetitiveness.

Conveying fiber optic links along different courses and executing defensive measures can moderate the effect of unanticipated occasions. Moreover, the improvement of quick reaction and reclamation methodologies is fundamental to limit margin time and keep up with the dependability of fiber optic organizations notwithstanding surprising disturbances.

Tending to the test of versatility is pivotal for the fate of fiber optics, particularly as information requests keep on raising dramatically. Guaranteeing that fiber optic organizations can oblige the developing number of associated gadgets, expanding information traffic, and advancing innovations requires proactive preparation and foundation plan. Versatility contemplations ought to include the actual parts of organization extension as well as the advancement of conventions and models that can consistently adjust to changing requests without compromising execution.

Taking everything into account, while the fate of fiber optics holds gigantic potential for changing ventures and empowering extraordinary network, there are multi-layered difficulties and contemplations that should be tended to. Online protection, cost, similarity with existing framework, the deficiency of gifted work force, natural effect, administrative cycles, restrictions in signal transmission, the transaction with remote advances, versatility to disturbances, and adaptability are among the key factors that will shape the direction of fiber optics in the years to come. A cooperative and vital methodology, including legislatures, industry partners, specialists, and the more extensive local area, is fundamental to beat these difficulties and open the maximum capacity of fiber optics as a foundation innovation in the computerized age.

6.4 Potential challenges and considerations for the future

As we diagram the course for the fate of fiber optics, it is pivotal to recognize and address likely difficulties and contemplations that might shape the direction of this groundbreaking innovation. The consistent joining of fiber optics into different enterprises and applications delivers a range of intricacies, from online protection worries to ecological contemplations. Exploring these difficulties requires a comprehensive and ground breaking way to deal with guarantee the proceeded with progress and development of fiber optic innovations.

Network safety arises as a central thought for the eventual fate of fiber optics. As the volume of information communicated through fiber optic organizations develops dramatically, the need to defend these organizations against digital dangers turns out to be progressively basic. Cybercriminals, with consistently advancing strategies, may take advantage of weaknesses in fiber optic frameworks to acquire unapproved admittance to delicate data, upset basic administrations, or participate in surveillance. The honesty and classification of information sent through fiber optics should be sustained through hearty encryption strategies, secure organization designs, and persistent checking. Cooperative endeavors between industry partners, online protection specialists, and administrative bodies are basic to remain in front of arising digital dangers and sustain the digital safeguards of fiber optic organizations.

The growing job of fiber optics in basic areas enhances the meaning of online protection contemplations. In medical services, where fiber optics are progressively utilized for high velocity and secure information transmission, the likely split the difference of patient information could have serious ramifications for protection and clinical honesty. Likewise, monetary organizations depend on fiber optics for fast and secure exchanges, making them possible focuses for digital assaults focused on monetary disturbances. A proactive and cooperative methodology, including public and confidential areas, is fundamental for strengthen online protection gauges and guarantee the flexibility of fiber optic organizations notwithstanding developing digital dangers.

While the advantages of fiber optics are significant, the forthright expenses related with sending fiber optic framework represent a critical test for broad reception. The underlying speculation expected for laying fiber optic links, particularly in districts or enterprises with restricted monetary assets, can go about as an impediment. Notwithstanding the drawn out benefits, including upgraded information move speeds and decreased support costs, imaginative funding models and motivators are expected to work with the reasonableness and openness of fiber optic innovations. Government drives, industry organizations, and global coordinated efforts might assume vital parts in tending to this test and advancing the far and wide sending of fiber optics.

Similarity issues with existing foundation address one more obstacle for the future reception of fiber optics. Changing from conventional copper-based frameworks to fiber optics might require significant adjustments or complete redesigns of existing foundation. Enterprises profoundly settled in heritage advances might confront disturbances during the progress, prompting possible margin time and efficiency misfortunes. A painstakingly arranged and staged coordination, combined with joint effort between partners, is fundamental to guarantee a smooth consolidation of fiber optics into different areas without compromising functional coherence.

The lack of gifted experts with mastery in fiber optics presents a test that could obstruct the consistent reception and support of fiber optic organizations. Introducing and keeping up with fiber optic foundation requests specific information and preparing. The flood popular for talented professionals, designers, and organization overseers capable in fiber optics is supposed to exceed the ongoing stockpile. Instructive establishments, industry players, and preparing programs should team up to foster far reaching drives that furnish people with the important abilities to configuration, introduce, and keep up with fiber optic organizations. Labor force improvement procedures and apprenticeship programs are urgent in tending to the lack of talented experts in the field of fiber optics.

Ecological contemplations are acquiring unmistakable quality in conversations encompassing innovation and foundation advancement. While fiber optics themselves are harmless to the ecosystem contrasted with customary copper links, the creation and removal of fiber optic parts have related ecological effects.

The assembling system includes energy utilization and natural substance extraction, adding to the general carbon impression. Also, the removal of obsolete or harmed fiber optic links might present ecological difficulties. The business must proactively investigate reasonable practices in fiber optic assembling, reusing programs, and naturally cognizant removal strategies to limit its biological impression.

The issue of option to proceed and the administrative system encompassing the establishment of fiber optic foundation is one more thought for what's to come. Getting the important authorizations and exploring administrative cycles can be tedious and complex. States and administrative bodies assume a significant part in smoothing out these cycles, guaranteeing that the organization of fiber optic organizations lines up with metropolitan preparation, natural guidelines, and local area interests. Cooperation between general society and confidential areas is vital for address administrative difficulties and work with the proficient extension of fiber optic framework.

The material science of light transmission through fiber optics forces constraints on signal misfortune over significant distances. While fiber optics offer unrivaled speed and data transfer capacity, conquering signal constriction challenges is a continuous area of innovative work. Advancements in enhancement innovations and sign recovery are critical to keep up with signal honesty and guarantee reliable execution, particularly as information requests keep on heightening. Proceeded with interest in propelling the capacities of fiber optic frameworks is vital for address the innate constraints and satisfy the developing needs for quicker and more dependable correspondence.

Signal obstruction and lessening because of outer elements, like curves, turns, or natural circumstances, address possible difficulties for the fate of fiber optics. The transmission of light signals through fiber optic links might be influenced by these elements, influencing signal quality and execution. Examination into materials and plans that limit signal constriction, combined with best practices in establishment and support, is basic for tending to these difficulties and guaranteeing dependable and predictable sign transmission.

The exchange between fiber optics and arising remote correspondence innovations presents a mind boggling scene for what's in store. While fiber optics offer unrivaled speed and dependability, the development of remote advancements, especially with regards to 6G and then some, may give elective answers for specific applications. Finding some kind of harmony between the qualities of fiber optics and the benefits presented by remote correspondence requires a nuanced way to deal with network plan and framework arranging. Half and half arrangements that join fiber optics with cutting edge remote advancements might arise as need might arise.

The potential for disturbances brought about by catastrophic events or mishaps represents a critical test for the fate of fiber optics. The actual weakness of fiber optic links to occasions like seismic tremors, floods, or development exercises requires strong making arrangements for network strength and overt repetitiveness. Sending fiber optic links along assorted courses, executing defensive measures, and creating quick reaction and rebuilding systems are fundamental to limit margin time and keep up with the unwavering quality of fiber optic organizations notwithstanding startling disturbances.

Versatility is a basic thought for the fate of fiber optics, particularly as information requests keep on raising. Guaranteeing that fiber optic organizations can oblige the developing number of associated gadgets, expanding information traffic, and advancing advancements requires proactive preparation and framework plan. Versatility contemplations ought to incorporate the actual parts of organization extension as well as the advancement of conventions and models that can consistently adjust to changing requests without compromising execution.

All in all, the eventual fate of fiber optics is overflowing with open doors, yet it likewise presents a range of difficulties and contemplations that request cautious consideration and key preparation. From network safety and cost limitations to similarity issues, ecological effect, and administrative contemplations, the diverse idea of these difficulties requires cooperative endeavors from states, industry partners, specialists, and the more extensive local area. Addressing these difficulties head-on is fundamental to opening the maximum capacity of fiber optics as a foundation innovation in the computerized age, forming the manner in which we convey, improve, and interface in the years to come.

Chapter 7

The Future of Web at Speed

The eventual fate of the web is unavoidably connected to the idea of speed. As we explore through the consistently developing scene of advanced innovation, the requirement for quicker and more effective web encounters turns out to be progressively obvious. The speed at which we can get to data, collaborate with applications, and consume content significantly affects our day to day routines, molding the manner in which we work, impart, and associate with the world.

One of the critical main impetuses behind the interest for speed is the developing intricacy of web applications and the rising dependence on information escalated processes. From web based superior quality recordings to running complex calculations progressively, present day web applications are pushing the limits of what was once imagined. Subsequently, clients have generally expected consistent and prompt cooperations, putting a top notch on the presentation of web stages.

The ascent of cell phones has additionally enhanced the significance of speed in the web environment. With a consistently developing number of clients getting to the web through cell phones and tablets, the requirement for responsive and quick stacking sites has become vital. Portable clients, specifically, request a frictionless encounter, and any deferrals or laziness can prompt dissatisfaction and withdrawal.

To address these difficulties and measure up to the rising assumptions of clients, the eventual fate of the web is being molded by a conversion of mechanical progressions and inventive methodologies. One of the significant components in this advancement is the continuous improvement of 5G innovation. As the fifth era of remote correspondence norms, 5G vows to convey uncommon speed and low inactivity, generally changing the manner in which we associate with the web.

The arrangement of 5G organizations is ready to upset the web insight, empowering quicker download and transfer speeds, decreased idleness, and further developed dependability. This shift towards 5G won't just help individual clients yet in addition open up additional opportunities for arising advances like the Web of Things (IoT), expanded reality (AR), and augmented reality (VR). The improved network given by 5G will be an impetus for another time of web applications and administrations that influence the capacities of these groundbreaking innovations.

Notwithstanding the progressions in remote correspondence, the fate of web speed is firmly entwined with the development of internet browsers. Program engineers are participated in a ceaseless competition to streamline execution and present highlights that improve the general client experience. One outstanding improvement in this area is the ascent of moderate web applications (PWAs), which consolidate the best of web and portable applications to offer quick, solid, and connecting with encounters.

PWAs influence current web capacities to convey application like encounters straightforwardly through the program. They are intended to work consistently across different gadgets and stages, killing the requirement for clients to download and introduce customary applications. The intrinsic speed and adaptability of PWAs pursue them a convincing decision for engineers and organizations hoping to give a frictionless encounter to their crowd.

Moreover, the approach of WebAssembly (Wasm) is reshaping the scene of web improvement and execution. WebAssembly is a twofold guidance design that empowers elite execution of code on internet browsers. By permitting designers to compose code in dialects, for example, C++ and Rust and run it at close local speed, WebAssembly makes the way for another time of web applications that can convey complex functionalities without forfeiting speed.

The mix of WebAssembly and other arising advances like Web Parts and GraphQL is driving a change in outlook in web improvement. Designers presently have the apparatuses and systems to construct exceptionally advanced and particular web applications that can adjust to the assorted necessities of clients. This adaptability is essential in a high speed computerized scene where client assumptions are continually developing.

In addition, the eventual fate of web speed is naturally connected to the idea of Edge Processing. Customarily, web applications have depended on incorporated servers to process and convey content. Be that as it may, as the interest for low-dormancy collaborations develops, the impediments of brought together handling become more obvious. Edge Figuring decentralizes computational assignments by finishing processing assets closer clients, diminishing inertness and further developing reaction times.

Edge Registering is especially important with regards to constant applications, for example, internet gaming, video conferencing, and cooperative apparatuses. By disseminating handling power across an organization of edge servers, these applications can convey close prompt reactions, making a more vivid and responsive client experience. The coordination of Edge Figuring with 5G innovation further upgrades the capacities of web applications, preparing for another period of dynamic and intelligent substance.

Man-made reasoning (artificial intelligence) and AI (ML) are likewise assuming an essential part in molding the eventual fate of web speed.

These advancements empower brilliant calculations that can dissect client conduct, foresee inclinations, and enhance content conveyance.

From customized suggestions to dynamic substance delivering, artificial intelligence and ML calculations are instrumental in making custom-made and elite execution web encounters.

Content Conveyance Organizations (CDNs) are one more foundation of web speed improvement. CDNs disperse content across an organization of servers decisively situated all over the planet. By storing and conveying content from servers that are geologically nearer to the client, CDNs diminish inactivity and speed up load times. The reconciliation of CDNs with arising advancements like edge figuring further upgrades their viability in improving web execution.

As the fate of the web unfurls, security stays a basic thought chasing speed. The rising refinement of digital dangers requires powerful safety efforts to shield client information and keep up with the respectability of web applications. The reception of HTTPS as the standard convention for secure correspondence is a demonstration of the business' obligation to focusing on client protection and information insurance.

The advancement of web speed isn't exclusively restricted to the domain of innovation. Client driven plan and openness are fundamental parts of a quick and comprehensive web. Plan rules that focus on effortlessness, lucidity, and instinctive route add to a positive client experience. Likewise, guaranteeing that web applications are available to clients with assorted capacities is a moral basic that lines up with the standards of inclusivity and balance.

All in all, the fate of the web at speed is a multi-layered venture that envelops mechanical development, client experience plan, and a promise to security and inclusivity. The intermingling of 5G, WebAssembly, Edge Processing, computer based intelligence, and other extraordinary advancements is reshaping the advanced scene, preparing for web encounters that are quicker, more responsive, and progressively refined.

As we explore this future, it is crucial for work out some kind of harmony among speed and the moral contemplations that support a mindful and comprehensive web. The continuous joint effort between engineers, organizations, and clients will be instrumental in forming a computerized biological system that fulfills the needs of speed as well as maintains the upsides of protection, security, and openness.

In this unique and steadily developing scene, the fate of the web isn't an objective yet a consistent excursion of development and variation. The difficulties and open doors that lie ahead will require an aggregate work to bridle the maximum capacity of arising innovations and guarantee that the web stays a strong and open instrument for people and organizations all over the planet.

7.1 Predictions for the future of internet speed and connectivity

The fate of web speed and network is ready for an extraordinary excursion, driven by mechanical headways, changing client assumptions, and the continuous development of computerized framework. As we peer into the distance, a few critical patterns and expectations arise, forming the scene of how we interface, convey, and consume data.

1. **5G Predominance and Then some:**
   The boundless arrangement and reception of 5G organizations are at the very front of expectations for the eventual fate of web speed. As the fifth era of remote innovation, 5G vows to convey unrivaled speed, diminished dormancy, and expanded network. The rollout of 5G organizations is supposed to be a distinct advantage, for individual clients as well as for organizations and ventures that depend on quick and solid web associations.

   Past 5G, the investigation of significantly further developed correspondence innovations is now in progress. Specialists and industry specialists are diving into the potential outcomes presented by 6G and then some, imagining networks that go past the abilities of 5G regarding rate, responsiveness, and by and large execution. These future cycles are probably going to present advancements, for example, terahertz correspondence and novel organization models, pushing the limits of what is as of now reachable.

2. **Edge Figuring's Ascendance:**
Edge Figuring is arising as a basic part in the journey for quicker web speeds and decreased dormancy. Conventional distributed computing depends on concentrated servers, which can present postpones in handling and conveying information. Edge Registering, in any case, decentralizes computational errands by carrying handling nearer to the information source, diminishing the distance data necessities to travel.

   This approach is especially significant for applications demanding continuous collaborations, like increased reality (AR), computer generated reality (VR), and internet gaming. As additional gadgets become associated, edge registering will assume a fundamental part in guaranteeing that information is handled quickly, adding to a more consistent and responsive web insight.

3. **Quantum Web Not too far off:**
Quantum registering has been a subject of interest in the tech world, and its possible effect on web speed and security is acquiring consideration. Quantum web, still in its earliest stages, plans to use the standards of quantum mechanics to empower super secure correspondence and quicker information transmission.

   In contrast to old style bits in customary registering, quantum bits or qubits can exist in different states at the same time, considering quicker calculation and transmission of data. The improvement of quantum web foundation is supposed to upset encryption strategies, making correspondences essentially unhackable.

   While viable execution is as of now a test, continuous examination and forward leaps recommend that quantum web could turn into a reality not long from now.

4. **Man-made reasoning in Organization Enhancement:**
Man-made brainpower (computer based intelligence) is set to assume a critical part in enhancing web speed and network. AI calculations can dissect immense measures of information to distinguish designs, foresee client conduct, and enhance network

execution. This proactive way to deal with network the executives guarantees that assets are allotted effectively, lessening blockage and upgrading in general speed.

Man-made intelligence fueled arrangements are likewise being utilized to distinguish and relieve network oddities, security dangers, and execution bottlenecks progressively. This prescient and versatile nature of simulated intelligence adds to a stronger and responsive web framework.

5. **Satellite Web for Worldwide Availability:**

   Satellite web is encountering a resurgence, driven by headways in satellite innovation and a developing interest for worldwide network. Organizations like SpaceX, OneWeb, and Amazon are putting resources into star groupings of low Earth circle (LEO) satellites to give fast web admittance to underserved and far off regions.

   These satellite heavenly bodies vow to convey low-idleness web associations, equaling or outperforming the paces presented by customary broadband suppliers. The potential for worldwide inclusion makes satellite web a central member in the mission to connect the computerized partition and carry rapid network to districts where customary foundation is trying to send.

6. **Web of Things (IoT) and Availability Requests:**

   The expansion of Web of Things (IoT) gadgets is reshaping availability necessities. As additional gadgets become associated, from savvy homes and wearable contraptions to modern sensors and independent vehicles, the interest for solid and quick web availability develops dramatically.

   The fate of web speed will be complicatedly connected to the capacity to oblige the assorted and synchronous associations produced by IoT gadgets. This requires quicker networks as well as further developed network the board capacities to deal with the special requests of IoT applications.

7. **Network Organizations and Decentralized Availability:**
Network organizations, where gadgets speak with one another as opposed to depending on a concentrated center point, are acquiring consideration as an expected answer for further developing web network. In a lattice organization, every gadget fills in as a hub that can hand-off information to different hubs, making a decentralized and versatile organization.

This approach can possibly upgrade availability in regions with restricted framework and empower dynamic variation to changing organization conditions. Network organizations could assume a critical part in stretching out web inclusion to distant areas and working on the general unwavering quality of web associations.

8. **Proceeded with Development of Fiber Optic Organizations:**
Fiber optic organizations have for quite some time been proclaimed for their capacity to give high velocity, dependable web associations. The continuous development of fiber optic foundation is a vital pattern in guaranteeing quicker and more predictable web speeds. Fiber optic links communicate information utilizing light signals, offering more prominent transmission capacity and lower inertness contrasted with conventional copper links.

Legislatures and media transmission organizations overall are putting resources into the sending of fiber optic organizations to bring gigabit-speed web to homes and organizations. The continuous endeavors to grow fiber optic framework are supposed to contribute fundamentally to the improvement of worldwide web network.

9. **Half breed and Multi-Cloud Approaches:**
The fate of web availability is probably going to be formed by half and half and multi-cloud draws near. As associations progressively take on cloud administrations for their processing needs, a mix of public and confidential mists, alongside on-premises framework, is turning into the standard. This half and half model considers more prominent adaptability, versatility, and overt repetitiveness.

Multi-cloud systems, where associations use administrations from different cloud suppliers, are likewise acquiring noticeable quality. This approach not just mitigates the gamble of dependence on a solitary supplier yet additionally empowers organizations to use the qualities of various cloud stages to upgrade execution and guarantee high accessibility.

10. **Administrative and Strategy Impacts:**

    The fate of web speed and network isn't just an innovative matter yet additionally likely to administrative and strategy impacts. States all over the planet assume a critical part in forming the computerized scene through guidelines, range portions, and interests in foundation.

    Internet fairness, the rule that network access suppliers ought to treat all information on the web the same way, without separating or charging diversely founded on client, content, or application, stays a subject of discussion. Administrative choices on internet fairness can affect the availability and speed of internet providers, molding the fate of how information is communicated and gotten.

11. **Green Web Drives:**

    As the world wrestles with natural difficulties, the manageability of web foundation is turning into a huge thought. The energy utilization of server farms and organization framework adds to fossil fuel byproducts, inciting the investigation of green web drives.

    Endeavors to plan energy-proficient server farms, advance organization equipment, and investigate environmentally friendly power hotspots for driving web foundation are picking up speed. The eventual fate of web speed might be interwoven with the business' obligation to harmless to the ecosystem works on, guaranteeing that the computerized development happens mindfully.

12. **Protection and Security Goals:**

In a time of expanding availability, the significance of protection and security couldn't possibly be more significant. The eventual fate of web speed will be molded by the execution of vigorous safety efforts to safeguard client information and guarantee the uprightness of online interchanges.

The boundless reception of encoded correspondence conventions, progressions in blockchain innovation, and the joining of secure equipment components are adding to a safer web climate. Adjusting the requirement for speed with tough protection and safety efforts will be a vital thought in the development of web network.

All in all, the fate of web speed and network is a dynamic and multi-layered scene molded by mechanical developments, client requests, administrative choices, and ecological contemplations. The continuous organization of 5G, investigation of quantum web, ascent of edge processing, and development of fiber optic organizations are demonstrative of the assorted ways that the advanced future might take.

7.2 Ongoing research and developments in fiber optic technology

Continuous examination and improvements in fiber optic innovation are at the front of the broadcast communications upset, molding how information is sent, empowering quicker web speeds, and upgrading the dependability of correspondence organizations. Fiber optic innovation, which utilizations beats of light to send information over slight strands of glass or plastic filaments, has gone through constant advancement to satisfy the rising needs for data transfer capacity, decreased inactivity, and further developed proficiency.

1. **Upgraded Information Transmission Velocities:**
   One of the essential areas of progressing research in fiber optic innovation spins around accomplishing considerably higher information transmission speeds. As the interest for quicker web and more effective correspondence networks keeps on developing, specialists are investigating ways of expanding the limit of existing fiber optic frameworks. This includes creating progressed

regulation methods, improving sign handling calculations, and investigating the utilization of new materials to upgrade the speed at which information can be communicated through fiber optic links.

As of late, analysts have taken critical steps in expanding the information paces of fiber optic correspondence. The arrangement of cutting edge adjustment plans, like quadrature plentifulness tweak (QAM), empowers the encoding of additional information inside each beat of light. Also, the advancement of cognizant correspondence frameworks has worked on the proficiency of information transmission over significant distances, adding to the acknowledgment of quicker and more dependable fiber optic organizations.

2. **Cutting edge Fiber Optic Links:**

Progressing research in fiber optic innovation reaches out to the advancement of cutting edge fiber optic links with further developed execution attributes. This incorporates the investigation of new materials for the fiber center and cladding, as well as progressions in the assembling cycles to decrease signal misfortunes and improve signal quality.

One remarkable area of examination is the improvement of multicore filaments, which highlight different centers inside a solitary fiber. This takes into account equal information transmission, altogether expanding the general information limit of the fiber optic link. Multicore filaments can possibly reform information transmission by giving a versatile answer for satisfy the consistently developing need for higher data transfer capacity.

Scientists are likewise researching the utilization of novel materials, like empty main elements, to diminish signal bends and misfortunes. Empty main elements can direct light more productively, limiting the effect of outer variables on signal quality. These headways in fiber configuration add to the improvement of additional vigorous and flexible fiber optic links for assorted applications.

3. **Quantum Correspondence and Cryptography:**
The field of quantum correspondence and cryptography addresses a state of the art area of exploration inside fiber optic innovation. Quantum correspondence use the standards of quantum mechanics to get the transmission of data, giving exceptional degrees of safety.

Quantum key dissemination (QKD) is a vital application in quantum correspondence. It includes the utilization of quantum properties to empower the solid trade of encryption keys between parties. Fiber optic channels assume an essential part in executing QKD frameworks, and progressing research expects to expand the span and productivity of quantum-got correspondence over fiber optic organizations.

The advancement of quantum repeaters is one more area of concentration. Quantum repeaters can expand the scope of quantum correspondence over significant distances, beating the restrictions forced by signal corruption. Specialists are investigating novel methodologies, like the utilization of ensnared photons and quantum recollections, to make more effective and down to earth quantum repeaters for joining into fiber optic foundation.

4. **Fiber Optic Detecting and IoT Applications:**
Past customary correspondence, progressing research in fiber optic innovation stretches out to detecting applications, with likely ramifications for the Web of Things (IoT) and different ventures. Fiber optic sensors influence the properties of light to recognize changes in temperature, strain, pressure, and other natural variables along the length of the fiber.

These sensors find applications in different businesses, including medical services, foundation checking, and ecological detecting. For instance, appropriated fiber optic sensors can be utilized to screen the underlying strength of extensions or distinguish spills in pipelines. Progressing research means to work on the awareness, exactness, and adaptability of fiber optic detecting advances to widen their pertinence in different fields.

The combination of fiber optic detecting with IoT gadgets is an area of investigation. By consolidating the abilities of fiber optic sensors with the interconnected idea of IoT, specialists imagine making savvy frameworks prepared to do constant checking and information driven independent direction. This union can possibly improve the proficiency and unwavering quality of basic foundation and modern cycles.

5. **Fiber Optic Organizations for 5G and Then some:**

The arrangement of 5G organizations and the expectation of future remote correspondence guidelines are driving continuous examination in fiber optic innovation. Fiber optic organizations structure the spine for supporting the rapid and low-dormancy prerequisites of 5G network. As the interest for information escalated applications and the quantity of associated gadgets keep on rising, scientists are centered around improving fiber optic organizations to meet these developing requirements.

One area of examination includes the advancement of fiber optic fronthaul and backhaul answers for 5G organizations. Fronthaul alludes to the association between the unified handling unit (computer chip) and the radio units at cell locales, while backhaul includes the association between various cell destinations and the center organization. Fiber optic answers for fronthaul and backhaul assume a significant part in guaranteeing the consistent and fast transmission of information inside the 5G foundation.

The appearance of future correspondence norms, frequently alluded to as 6G and then some, presents new difficulties and valuable open doors for fiber optic innovation. Specialists are investigating imaginative ways to deal with additional improve the limit, speed, and adaptability of fiber optic organizations to help the expected necessities of future remote correspondence frameworks.

6. **Energy Proficiency and Supportability:**
As the significance of natural supportability acquires unmistakable quality, continuous examination in fiber optic innovation incorporates endeavors to further develop the energy proficiency of fiber optic organizations.

Energy utilization in server farms and media transmission framework is a critical concern, and scientists are investigating ways of decreasing the power prerequisites of fiber optic frameworks.

Endeavors to plan energy-proficient parts, like low-power handsets and speakers, add to limiting the natural effect of fiber optic organizations. Furthermore, headways in network the board calculations and conventions mean to advance the utilization of assets, lessening superfluous energy utilization in fiber optic correspondence.

The joining of sustainable power sources, for example, sunlight based or wind power, into fiber optic organization foundation is additionally an area of investigation. Reasonable practices in the plan, sending, and activity of fiber optic organizations are fundamental for making an all the more harmless to the ecosystem and energy-productive media communications biological system.

7. **Simulated intelligence Driven Organization Streamlining:**
The convergence of fiber optic innovation and man-made consciousness (computer based intelligence) presents open doors for streamlining network execution and guaranteeing effective asset use. Man-made intelligence calculations can examine tremendous measures of information from fiber optic organizations progressively, empowering prescient upkeep, proactive shortcoming identification, and dynamic asset designation.

Man-made intelligence driven network streamlining adds to the dependability and responsiveness of fiber optic correspondence. By wisely overseeing network traffic, foreseeing likely disappointments, and adjusting to evolving conditions, simulated intelligence improves the general effectiveness of fiber optic frameworks. Progressing research in this space centers around refining computer based intelligence models, creating progressed examination apparatuses, and coordinating simulated intelligence driven arrangements into existing fiber optic foundation.

8. **Biocompatible Fiber Optics for Clinical Applications:**

   In the domain of clinical applications, continuous exploration investigates the improvement of biocompatible fiber optics for different analytic and restorative purposes. Fiber optic tests and sensors that can be securely brought into the human body offer additional opportunities for insignificantly intrusive operations and constant checking of physiological boundaries.

   Biocompatible fiber optics track down applications in clinical imaging, endoscopy, and detecting inside the human body. Analysts are dealing with working on the adaptability, biocompatibility, and imaging capacities of these strands to empower exact and safe clinical intercessions. The joining of fiber optic innovation with clinical gadgets holds guarantee for propelling medical services rehearses and working on quiet results.

9. **Normalization and Interoperability:**

   Normalization and interoperability are basic parts of continuous examination in fiber optic innovation. As the utilization of fiber optic organizations becomes universal across different applications and businesses, the requirement for normalized conventions and connection points becomes principal. Normalization endeavors intend to guarantee similarity between various parts, gadgets, and frameworks, cultivating a firm and interoperable biological system.

   The improvement of industry norms for fiber optic correspondence, for example, those set by associations like the Worldwide Media transmission Association (ITU) and the Organization of Electrical and Hardware Designers (IEEE), guides continuous examination in making bound together arrangements. Interoperability testing and confirmation processes assume a urgent part in laying out a typical structure for the sending of fiber optic innovation across different applications.

10. **Beating Distance and Sign Misfortune Difficulties:**
    Regardless of the intrinsic benefits of fiber optic innovation, challenges connected with signal misfortune and distance impediments continue. Continuous examination looks to address these difficulties through advancements in signal enhancement, scattering the executives, and the improvement of cutting edge fiber optic parts.

    Intensification methods, for example, the utilization of erbium-doped fiber enhancers (EDFAs), expect to help signals over significant distances without compromising sign quality. Research endeavors likewise center around relieving signal contortions brought about by variables, for example, chromatic scattering and polarization mode scattering, which can affect the trustworthiness of communicated information.

    Progressions in nonlinear optics and specialty filaments add to conquering distance and sign misfortune challenges. Nonlinear optical impacts, for example, four-wave blending and self-stage tweak, are areas of investigation for upgrading the presentation of fiber optic frameworks overstretched distances. Continuous exploration in specialty strands, including photonic precious stone filaments and microstructured strands, expects to make custom fitted arrangements that address explicit difficulties related with signal transmission.

11. **Space-Based Fiber Optic Correspondence:**
    Research in fiber optic innovation reaches out past the bounds of the World's surface, with investigation into space based fiber optic correspondence. The remarkable difficulties of room correspondence, including the impacts of microgravity and radiation, require specific answers for solid and fast information

transmission.

Satellites outfitted with fiber optic innovation hold the possibility to upset space-based correspondence. Continuous exploration includes creating space-viable fiber optic parts, links, and frameworks to guarantee the consistent exchange of information among Earth and

space-based resources. The joining of fiber optics in space-based correspondence networks adds to the acknowledgment of cutting edge satellite correspondence frameworks and profound space investigation missions.

12. **Online protection and Secure Fiber Optic Correspondence:**

With the rising significance of secure correspondence, continuous exploration in fiber optic innovation incorporates endeavors to improve the online protection parts of fiber optic organizations. Secure correspondence over fiber optics is critical for shielding delicate information from block attempt and unapproved access.

Scientists are investigating cryptographic arrangements custom fitted for fiber optic correspondence to guarantee the secrecy and honesty of communicated information. Quantum key circulation, as referenced prior with regards to quantum correspondence, is an eminent illustration of a solid specialized strategy that use the standards of quantum mechanics to accomplish rugged encryption.

Fiber optic links are defenseless against actual tapping, and exploration centers around creating alter apparent and alter safe answers for identify and forestall unapproved access. Also, progressions in interruption discovery frameworks and encryption advances add to the general security stance of fiber optic correspondence organizations.

7.3 Policy considerations and implications for widespread adoption

Strategy contemplations assume a vital part in molding the direction of mechanical developments, and the far reaching reception of arising advancements is no special case. As society explores the groundbreaking scenes introduced by headways in fields like computerized reasoning (computer based intelligence), biotechnology, and sustainable power, policymakers face the perplexing errand of creating viable and moral systems that offset development with the prosperity of people and society overall. Analyzing the strategy contemplations and suggestions for the broad reception of arising advances gives bits of knowledge into how social orders can outfit the advantages while alleviating possible dangers.

1. **Moral Systems and Dependable Development:**
   One of the preeminent arrangement contemplations for boundless reception rotates around laying out vigorous moral systems and advancing dependable advancement. As innovations quickly develop, moral rules give an ethical compass to engineers, organizations, and policymakers. Questions encompassing issues like security, predisposition in simulated intelligence calculations, and the moral ramifications of hereditary designing interest smart thought.
   Policymakers should team up with specialists, industry partners, and general society to form moral norms that guide the turn of events and sending of arising advancements.
   Moral contemplations stretch out past unambiguous advances to incorporate more extensive cultural effects, guaranteeing that development lines up with values like value, straightforwardness, and common liberties. By encouraging a culture of capable development, policymakers can assist with building trust and trust in the far reaching reception of extraordinary advancements.

2. **Security and Information Insurance:**
   The coming of advanced advancements has introduced a period of exceptional information age and assortment. In that capacity, security and information assurance are basic approach contemplations for the far reaching reception of advancements like simulated intelligence, IoT (Web of Things), and information

examination. Policymakers should lay out clear guidelines to shield people's protection, control the way in which their information is utilized, and guarantee straightforwardness in information rehearses.

Systems like the Overall Information Security Guideline (GDPR) in the European Association act as models for complete information security arrangements. Finding some kind of harmony between working with development and safeguarding people's protection privileges is a sensitive undertaking, requiring progressing variation as innovation advances. Policymakers need to work cooperatively with industry partners to plan structures that maintain protection principles while empowering the dependable utilization of information for cultural advantages.

3. **Openness and Computerized Incorporation:**

   As groundbreaking advancements become necessary to different parts of day to day existence, policymakers should focus on openness and computerized consideration. Guaranteeing that the advantages of development arrive at all sections of society is fundamental for forestalling the compounding of existing social incongruities. Strategies that address issues like the computerized partition, moderateness of innovation, and openness for people with inabilities add to a more comprehensive mechanical scene.

   Legislatures can carry out drives to give evenhanded admittance to schooling, preparing, and computerized foundation. This incorporates endeavors to overcome any issues in web access, advance computerized education, and cultivate inclusivity in the plan of innovation. Policymakers ought to team up with different partners to foster methodologies that engage minimized networks and advance equivalent cooperation in the open doors presented by arising advances.

4. **Network safety and Versatility:**

   The rising dependence on computerized advances elevates the significance of strong network safety arrangements to shield against digital dangers and assaults. The broad reception of advances, for example, distributed computing, IoT, and man-made intelligence presents new assault vectors and weaknesses.

Policymakers should zero in on creating and refreshing network safety systems to safeguard basic framework, delicate information, and people's protection.

Viable approaches ought to empower coordinated effort between government, industry, and network safety specialists to share danger insight and best practices. Network protection guidelines ought to likewise advance the improvement of secure-by-plan innovations, boost the reception of encryption gauges, and lay out occurrence reaction conventions. By focusing on network safety, policymakers add to the strength of mechanical biological systems and safeguard against possible interruptions.

5. **Administrative Sandboxes for Advancement:**

   To support trial and error and cultivate development, policymakers can lay out administrative sandboxes - controlled conditions that permit organizations to test new advancements and plans of action without promptly sticking to every single administrative necessity. Administrative sandboxes give a space to iterative testing, permitting controllers to notice this present reality ramifications of creative arrangements prior to executing more extensive strategies.

   By embracing administrative sandboxes, policymakers figure out some kind of harmony between cultivating advancement and safeguarding the public interest. These conditions empower new businesses and laid out organizations the same to investigate arising innovations, recognize possible difficulties, and team up with controllers to foster compelling and custom-made administrative systems. Policymakers can gain from sandbox analyses to illuminate proof based guidelines that help development while limiting dangers.

6. **Instruction and Labor force Improvement:**
   The broad reception of arising innovations requires a talented and versatile labor force. Policymakers should focus on instruction and labor force improvement arrangements that furnish people with the abilities expected to explore the computerized scene. Drives might incorporate curricular updates to integrate STEM (science, innovation, designing, and math) training, re-skilling programs for existing specialists, and coordinated efforts between instructive organizations and industry.

   Tending to the developing requests of the gig market requires prescience and proactive strategies that expect to arise ability prerequisites. Policymakers can boost public-private organizations, reserve research on labor force patterns, and execute arrangements that support consistent learning. By putting resources into training and labor force advancement, policymakers enable people to partake in and add to the development driven economy.

7. **Antitrust and Market Contest:**
   The grouping of force among a couple of predominant innovation organizations has raised worries about fair contest and market elements. Policymakers should consider antitrust guidelines that forestall monopolistic practices, advance contest, and guarantee a level battleground for organizations. This incorporates investigating consolidations and acquisitions that could smother contest and thwart development.

   Antitrust approaches ought to be adjusted to the advanced age, where information driven market predominance and stage biological systems can impact contest elements. Policymakers need to find some kind of harmony between taking into account sound contest and forestalling anticompetitive way of behaving. Compelling antitrust guidelines add to a different and cutthroat mechanical scene that benefits the two organizations and buyers.

8. **Licensed innovation and Development Motivators:**
   Licensed innovation (IP) strategies assume a vital part in boosting

development by safeguarding the privileges of designers and makers. Policymakers should constantly rethink IP structures to figure out some kind of harmony between encouraging advancement and forestalling the abuse of licensed innovation to smother contest. This incorporates thinking about the patentability of specific advances, tending to patent savages, and guaranteeing fair utilization of protected material.

Also, policymakers can investigate elective motivating force components, for example, open-source drives and cooperative examination models, to energize development while guaranteeing wide admittance to information. Making adaptable IP strategies that adjust to the developing idea of innovation advances a favorable climate for imagination and development.

9. **Ecological Supportability:**

The ecological effect of arising innovations is a basic thought for policymakers. From the creation of electronic gadgets to the energy utilization of server farms, the inescapable reception of innovation can add to biological difficulties. Policymakers should institute guidelines that advance maintainable practices, energy proficiency, and mindful waste administration inside the innovation area.

Drives might incorporate boosting the utilization of sustainable power in server farms, directing e-garbage removal, and empowering the improvement of eco-accommodating advances. By coordinating natural maintainability into strategy contemplations, policymakers add to the capable reception of innovation and address the biological impression related with advancement.

10. **Worldwide Joint effort and Administration:**

Given the worldwide idea of arising advances, policymakers should participate in global cooperation and administration endeavors. Normalizing works on, sharing experiences, and tending to worldwide difficulties require facilitated endeavors across borders. Policymakers can partake in global gatherings, team up on research drives, and lay out arrangements to guarantee a blended way to deal with the reception of arising innovations.

Issues, for example, cross-line information streams, worldwide network safety participation, and moral rules for worldwide computer based intelligence improvement request cooperative arrangements.

Policymakers ought to cooperate to lay out structures that work with moral and dependable development on a worldwide scale, cultivating a common obligation to the advantages and capable utilization of arising technology.

7.4 Closing thoughts on the transformative power of high-speed fiber optic internet

The extraordinary force of high velocity fiber optic web is reshaping the manner in which social orders associate, impart, and draw in with the computerized world. As we consider the effect of this trend setting innovation, it becomes clear that fiber optic web is something beyond a course for quicker information transmission — it is an impetus for development, financial development, and cultural advancement. In these end considerations, we dive into the complex ramifications of rapid fiber optic web and driving positive change across different domains potential.

1. **Speeding up Advanced Change:**
   High velocity fiber optic web fills in as the foundation of the advanced age, speeding up the speed of computerized change across enterprises. From organizations embracing distributed computing and constant coordinated effort to people taking part in consistent video conferencing and online training, the speed and dependability of fiber optic associations are essential empowering influences of a more associated and proficient computerized environment. The extraordinary effect is clear in the manner associations influence computerized devices, streamline processes, and

convey creative arrangements, eventually encouraging a dynamic and tough advanced economy.

2. **Connecting the Metropolitan Provincial Computerized Gap:**
One of the surprising parts of fast fiber optic web is crossing over the computerized split among metropolitan and country areas potential. By and large, rustic networks confronted difficulties in getting to fast web, restricting their capacity to take part completely in the advanced economy. Fiber optic foundation offers a versatile and future-verification arrangement that can stretch out rapid web network to underserved locales. By limiting the metropolitan country advanced hole, fiber optic web adds to rise to valuable open doors for schooling, medical services, and financial investment, encouraging comprehensive development and diminishing differences.

3. **Enabling Advancement and Business venture:**
The extraordinary force of fiber optic web stretches out to its part in enabling advancement and business venture. Fast, low-inactivity associations give a fruitful ground to new companies and trailblazers to investigate arising innovations, foster new applications, and team up on weighty ventures. The openness of fiber optic web foundation supports a culture of development by bringing hindrances down to section and working with the trading of thoughts. This strengthening of enterprising undertakings adds to work creation, monetary expansion, and the rise of lively advanced biological systems.

4. **Reforming Medical care Conveyance:**
In the domain of medical services, high velocity fiber optic web is an impetus for changing the conveyance of clinical benefits. Telemedicine, empowered by vigorous and solid web associations, permits medical care experts to direct far off counsels, screen patients progressively, and share clinical data consistently. The extraordinary effect is especially clear in provincial or distant regions where admittance to specific medical care administrations

might be restricted. Fiber optic web adds to the advancement of shrewd medical services arrangements, making ready for more available, productive, and patient-driven medical care conveyance models.

5. **Upgrading Instructive Open doors:**
The instructive scene goes through a significant change with the coming of rapid fiber optic web. From web based learning stages and virtual homerooms to intelligent instructive assets, fiber optic associations give the transfer speed and unwavering quality expected to help inventive educating and learning techniques. This change is especially critical with regards to separate training, deep rooted learning, and expertise improvement. By upgrading instructive open doors, fiber optic web assumes a significant part in molding the information economy and planning people for the difficulties of a quickly developing computerized world.

6. **Cultivating Brilliant Urban communities and Framework:**
The idea of savvy urban areas, described by proficient metropolitan foundation, feasible practices, and upgraded personal satisfaction, depends intensely on cutting edge network. Rapid fiber optic web shapes the foundation of brilliant city drives, supporting interconnected frameworks like savvy transportation, energy the board, and public administrations. The organization of fiber optic organizations empowers the joining of sensors, information examination, and continuous correspondence, cultivating a more responsive and economical metropolitan climate. The groundbreaking capability of fiber optic web reaches out to the improvement of savvy framework that upgrades effectiveness, versatility, and generally speaking metropolitan living encounters.

7. **Reinforcing Public Intensity:**
In the globalized computerized economy, a country's seriousness is unpredictably connected to the quality and reach of its computerized foundation. Rapid fiber optic web upgrades a country's computerized capacities, situating it as a cutthroat

player on the worldwide stage. Nations that put resources into fiber optic organizations exhibit a promise to encouraging development, drawing in ventures, and empowering a flourishing computerized environment. The extraordinary effect is apparent in the manner countries influence progressed network to drive financial development, draw in ability, and position themselves as center points for mechanical advancement.

8. **Strength Despite Difficulties:**
The strength of high velocity fiber optic web framework turns out to be especially vital in the midst of unanticipated difficulties, like catastrophic events or worldwide disturbances. The dependability and overt repetitiveness innate in fiber optic organizations add to the coherence of fundamental administrations, crisis correspondences, and fiasco reaction endeavors. The groundbreaking force of fiber optic web isn't just in that frame of mind to improve day to day exercises yet additionally in its ability to give a vigorous and strong correspondence spine during testing conditions.

9. **Sustaining a Computerized Society:**
Fiber optic web assumes a urgent part in sustaining the development of a computerized society, where network is unavoidable, and computerized connections consistently coordinate into day to day existence. The extraordinary power reaches out to social collaborations, social trade, and municipal commitment worked with by rapid web associations. As social orders become progressively interconnected, the texture of day to day existence is woven with advanced strings, impacting the manner in which individuals impart, team up, and add to their networks.

10. **Ecological Contemplations and Supportability:**
While praising the extraordinary force of rapid fiber optic web, taking into account its natural ramifications and the more extensive setting of sustainability is pivotal. The arrangement and support of fiber optic foundation have related ecological expenses,

including the assembling of gear, energy utilization in server farms, and the effect of development exercises. Policymakers and industry partners should be mindful of manageability contemplations, looking to limit the carbon impression of rapid web framework through energy-effective advancements, sustainable power sources, and dependable organization rehearses.

11. **Network protection and Security Goals:**

As fast fiber optic web turns into a vital piece of the advanced scene, guaranteeing network safety and safeguarding client protection become basic strategy contemplations. The extraordinary force of cutting edge availability accompanies the obligation to shield against digital dangers, information breaks, and unapproved access. Policymakers should authorize vigorous network safety guidelines, advance encryption rehearses, and lay out structures for client security insurance. The harmony between cultivating development and saving security and protection is a fragile one, and compelling strategies add to building a reliable and secure computerized climate.

12. **Cooperative Administration for an Associated Future:**

In exploring the groundbreaking scene of high velocity fiber optic web, cooperative administration arises as a key subject. Policymakers, industry pioneers, technologists, and the general population should take part in continuous exchanges, sharing experiences, and aggregately forming the arrangements that administer advanced availability.

The extraordinary force of fiber optic web is certainly not a performance try; it requires a cooperative and comprehensive way to deal with address different viewpoints, expect difficulties, and cultivate a climate where the advantages of cutting edge network are shared fairly.

Fast fiber optic web remains at the front of the computerized unrest, introducing another period of availability described by remarkable speed, unwavering quality, and groundbreaking potential. As we dive into the complexities of rapid fiber optic web, it becomes obvious that this innovation is in excess of a conductor for sending information — it is an impetus for development, monetary development, and cultural headway. In this investigation, we will disentangle the key parts, mechanical underpinnings, and broad ramifications of high velocity fiber optic web.

1. **Innovative Groundworks of Fiber Optic Web:**
   At the center of fast fiber optic web is the central rule of communicating information utilizing beats of light through slim strands of glass or plastic filaments. Not at all like customary copper-based frameworks, which depend on electrical signs, fiber optic links bridle the speed and effectiveness of light. This optical transmission of information empowers fundamentally higher transfer speeds, quicker information rates, and decreased signal corruption over significant distances.

   The critical parts of a fiber optic framework incorporate the transmitter, the fiber optic link itself, and the beneficiary. The transmitter changes over electrical signs into optical signs, which are then sent through the fiber optic link. These links comprise of a center (where the light voyages), cladding (which mirrors the light inside the center), and an external defensive layer. The collector at the opposite finish of the framework changes over the optical signs once more into electrical signs for translation by electronic gadgets.

2. **Releasing Exceptional Rates:**
   The essential appeal of rapid fiber optic web lies in its capacity to convey information at speeds that dominate conventional broadband advancements. Fiber optic links can send information at the speed of light, offering gigabit and even terabit speeds. This unprecedented speed converts into quick downloads, consistent video web based, and low-idleness associations, reclassifying client encounters and assumptions in the advanced domain.

   The speed benefits of fiber optic web are especially eminent in situations where enormous volumes of information should be communicated rapidly and dependably. Applications, for example, internet gaming, superior quality video conferencing, and gigantic information moves for organizations benefit colossally from the quick information transmission abilities of fiber optic innovation.

3. **Low Inertness and High Unwavering quality:**
Idleness, the deferral among sending and getting information, is a basic calculate deciding the responsiveness of web associations. Fiber optic web succeeds in limiting dormancy because of the speed of light transmission and the productivity of optical signs. This trademark is particularly urgent for ongoing applications, for example, web based gaming, video conferencing, and monetary exchanges, where postponements can fundamentally affect client experience.

Also, fiber optic links show high unwavering quality and flexibility to outside obstruction. Dissimilar to customary copper links, which are vulnerable to electromagnetic obstruction and sign debasement over significant distances, fiber optics keep up with signal honesty overstretched courses. This strength adds to a steady and trustworthy web association, diminishing the probability of blackouts or administration disturbances.

4. **Transmission capacity Development for Developing Information Requests:**
In the period of information concentrated applications, the interest for higher data transfer capacity keeps on flooding. Fast fiber optic web fulfills this need by giving extensive data transmission limits that far outperform those of customary broadband advances. The capacity to communicate an immense measure of information at the same time empowers consistent performing multiple tasks, upholds superior quality video web based, and obliges the thriving prerequisites of the Web of Things (IoT) and shrewd gadgets.

As the computerized scene develops with the rise of 4K and 8K video, computer generated reality, expanded reality, and different information hungry applications, the versatility of fiber optic organizations positions them as a future-evidence answer for address raising transfer speed needs. This adaptability is accomplished by utilizing progressed multiplexing strategies, for example, frequency division multiplexing (WDM), which permits numerous signs to travel simultaneously along various frequencies inside a similar fiber optic link.

5. **Empowering 5G Availability and Then some:**
The coming of fifth-age (5G) remote innovation proclaims another period of network described by super quick rates, low idleness, and backing for a monstrous number of synchronous associations. High velocity fiber optic web assumes a vital part in empowering 5G availability by filling in as the spine foundation for 5G organizations. Fiber optic associations give the vital ability to help the high information throughput and low-idleness necessities of 5G applications.

As the world looks past 5G toward people in the future of remote correspondence, fiber optic web stays a key part in the development of network norms. The advancement of 6G and past imagines considerably quicker information rates, vivid expanded reality encounters, and pervasive availability. Fiber optic organizations, with their inborn abilities for fast information transmission, will be indispensable to understanding the aggressive objectives of future remote correspondence frameworks.

6. **Fiber to the Home (FTTH) and Last-Mile Availability:**
The vision of bringing rapid fiber optic web straightforwardly to homes and organizations is acknowledged through Fiber to the Home (FTTH) or Fiber to the Premises (FTTP) arrangements. FTTH includes broadening fiber optic associations from focal trades or server farms straightforwardly to individual homes or business foundations, disposing of the requirement for copper-

based last-mile associations.

FTTH addresses a change in outlook in web network, offering balanced speeds for both transfers and downloads. This is as a distinct difference to conventional broadband innovations, which frequently furnish uneven velocities with more slow transfer rates. The arrangement of FTTH upgrades the client experience as well as future-verifications the foundation, obliging the developing interest for upstream transmission capacity driven by satisfied creation, video conferencing, and cloud-based applications.

7. **Monetary and Social Effects:**

The monetary and social effects of fast fiber optic web are significant, affecting different aspects of society. Monetarily, the arrangement of fiber optic organizations adds to work creation, animates financial development, and upgrades the seriousness of areas that put resources into cutting edge availability. Organizations, especially those in the innovation, development, and computerized areas, benefit from the high velocity, dependable web that empowers them to work effectively, arrive at worldwide business sectors, and advance quickly.

On a cultural level, admittance to rapid web encourages computerized consideration and diminishes differences in schooling, medical services, and financial open doors. Fiber optic availability in provincial and underserved regions opens up additional opportunities for remote work, distance learning, and telehealth administrations. The democratization of fast web access enables people and networks, giving them the apparatuses and assets to take part completely in the advanced age.

8. **Difficulties and Contemplations:**

While the extraordinary force of high velocity fiber optic web is clear, the arrangement and far reaching reception of this innovation are not without challenges. The forthright expenses related with laying fiber optic framework, particularly for FTTH organizations, can be significant. Policymakers, industry partners, and legislatures need to team up to address the monetary hindrances and foster methodologies for boosting interests in fiber optic organizations.

Administrative contemplations likewise assume a urgent part in molding the scene of fiber optic web. Policymakers should lay out clear systems that work with the sending of fiber optic foundation, address issues of option to proceed access, and advance sound contest on the lookout. Moreover, guaranteeing that fast web access is reasonable and open to all fragments of society is a key test that requires proactive strategies and inventive arrangements.

9. **Future Developments and Quantum Web:**
Looking forward, the eventual fate of rapid fiber optic web is interlaced with progressing advancements and the investigation of state of the art innovations. Quantum web, which use the standards of quantum mechanics to empower super secure correspondence, addresses an outskirts in the development of network. Scientists are investigating the improvement of quantum correspondence networks that could rethink the security and protection guidelines of web correspondence.

While quantum web is in the beginning phases of innovative work, its capability to supplement and upgrade existing fiber optic foundation is a subject of developing interest. The incorporation of quantum key dispersion (QKD) conventions into fiber optic organizations holds the commitment of accomplishing solid encryption, shielding against the dangers presented by quantum PCs to customary cryptographic strategies.

10. **Worldwide Availability and Submarine Fiber Optic Links:**
The worldwide availability worked with by high velocity fiber optic web reaches out underneath the oceans, where submarine fiber optic links mismatch the sea floor, associating landmasses and empowering intercontinental information transmission. Submarine links are the foundation of global web network, working

with the trading of information between locales with surprising rate and productivity.

The organization and upkeep of submarine links present novel difficulties, including the requirement for particular boats and hardware to lay links across immense maritime spreads. Be that as it may, the advantages of worldwide network are enormous, cultivating global cooperation, empowering constant correspondence, and supporting the consistent progression of data across borders. As advanced globalization proceeds, submarine fiber optic links will assume an undeniably crucial part in forming the interconnected universe representing things to come.

11. **Online protection and Security Objectives:**

The fast multiplication of rapid fiber optic web likewise delivers network safety and security objectives that request cautious thought. With the rising dependence on computerized network for basic foundation, interchanges, and individual connections, shielding against digital dangers becomes central. Policymakers and industry partners should team up to institute powerful network safety guidelines, execute encryption principles, and lay out structures for safeguarding client protection.

The weaknesses related with high velocity web, including the potential for Disseminated Refusal of Administration (DDoS) assaults, information breaks, and other digital dangers, require proactive measures to sustain the strength of fiber optic organizations. Continuous innovative work in network protection innovations, danger knowledge sharing, and the reception of best practices are necessary parts of a complete way to deal with getting fast fiber optic web.

12. **Ecological Contemplations and Maintainability:**

As the organization of high velocity fiber optic web grows, contemplations of ecological manageability come to the very front. The assembling of fiber optic links, the energy utilization of server farms, and the development exercises related with laying fiber optic framework all add to the natural impression of this innovation. Policymakers and industry pioneers should be mindful of these natural contemplations and endeavor to limit the environmental effect of high velocity web organizations.

Developments in energy-proficient advancements, the utilization of environmentally friendly power hotspots for server farms, and dependable organization practices can add to the manageability of fiber optic web. Adjusting the advantages of cutting edge network with ecological stewardship is a basic part of guaranteeing that the extraordinary force of fast fiber optic web lines up with more extensive objectives of manageability and capable innovation organization.

www.ingramcontent.com/pod-product-compliance
Lightning Source LLC
LaVergne TN
LVHW021238080526
838199LV00088B/4573